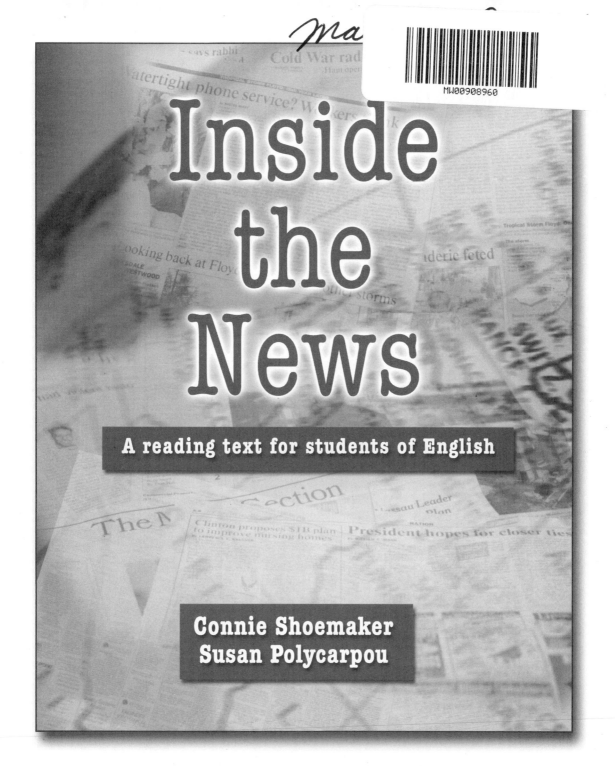

Inside
the
News

A reading text for students of English

Connie Shoemaker
Susan Polycarpou

Harcourt College Publishers

Fort Worth   Philadelphia   San Diego   New York   Orlando   Austin   San Antonio
Toronto   Montreal   London   Sydney   Tokyo

Publisher	Phyllis Dobbins
Acquisitions Editor	Kurk Gayle
Marketing Strategist	Jill Yuen
Project Manager	Angela Williams Urquhart

Photo Credits: Page 1: Habitat for Humanity International; Pages 6, 33, 50, 67, 75, 87, and 94: A/P Wide World Photos; Page 11: Rocky Mountain Adventures, Inc.; Page 18: Essadras M. Suarez, Denver Rocky Mountain News; Page 19: GARFIELD©1998 Paws, Inc. Reprinted with permission of Universal Press Syndicate. All rights reserved.; Pages 21 and 28: Connie Shoemaker; Pages 39 and 72: Digital Imagery ©2000 PhotoDisc, Inc.; Page 43: 2000 Peter Menzel. Image is from the book *Robo sapiens: Evolution of a New Species*. Peter Menzel and Faith D'Aluiso. A Material World Book. The MIT Press. 2000; Page 55: Hal Stoelzle, Denver Rocky Mountain News; Page 62: Mark Bonifacio, New York Daily News; Page 82: Kristine Larsen 2000; Page 99: The Seattle Times; Page 106: Mark H. Hunter, Hunter Studios

Cover Photo: Digital Vision, Ltd.

Cover Design: Robert Bovasso

ISBN: 0-15-506435-5

Library of Congress Card Number: 00-110840

Address for Domestic Orders
Harcourt College Publishers, 6277 Sea Harbor Drive, Orlando, FL 32887-6777
800-782-4479

Address for International Orders
International Customer Service
Harcourt College Publishers, 6277 Sea Harbor Drive, Orlando, FL 32887-6777
407-345-3800
(fax) 407-345-4060
(e-mail) hbintl@harcourtbrace.com

Address for Editorial Correspondence
Harcourt College Publishers, 301 Commerce Street, Suite 3700, Fort Worth, TX 76102

Web Site Address
http://www.harcourtcollege.com

Printed in the United States of America

1 2 3 4 5 6 7 8 9   039   9 8 7 6 5 4 3 2

Harcourt College Publishers

Dedication

To the many students who helped us develop and classroom test *Inside the News,* especially Ayoub, German, Kazuhiro, Maziad, Mido, and Salem.

Literary Credits

We wish to credit the following sources for story ideas:

Chapter One: Page 2, "Group Helps Others to Build Houses," Habitat for Humanity Website (www.habitat.org), Feb. 8, 1998; Page 6, "Frenchman's Dream Apartment Turns into Nightmare," *Reader's Digest,* by Pierre-Yves Glass, August 1996, from Associated Press.
Chapter Two: Page 12, "Fast Pigeons Help Photographer," *Adventure News,* April 1996; Page 18, "Dog Is Girl's Bridge to the World," by Lisa Levitt Rychman, Dec. 25, 1996.
Chapter Three: Page 22, "Dolls Teach What It's Like to Be Parents," *The Rocky Mountain News,* by Sam Omatsaye, October 21, 1997; Page 28, "Students Learn at Home in On-Line School," Associated Press, December 2, 1997, from CNN Interactive (www.cnn.com).
Chapter Four: Page 34, "McDonald's Opens New Delhi Restaurant," Associated Press, by Donna Bryson, October 14, 1996; Page 39, "Hot Climates and Hot Food Go Together," *The Denver Post,* Jane Brody, March 2, 1998.
Chapter Five: Page 44, "This Robot Loves People," by Douglas Whynott, *Discover,* October 1999; Page 50, "Cockroaches Become Robots," Associated Press, by Eric Talmadge, January 10, 1997.
Chapter Six: Page 56, "Neighbor Children Are Mighty Heroes," *The Rocky Mountain News,* by James B. Meadow, December 18, 1996; Page 62, "Falling Boy Bounces Off Woman," Associated Press, April 2, 1998.
Chapter Seven: Page 68, "Gorilla Saves Little Boy," *The Washington Post,* by Kathy Sawyer, August 24, 1996.
Chapter Eight: Page 76, "Basketball Stars Become Hip-Hop Singers," *The New York Times Upfront Magazine,* by Chris Broussard, December 13, 1999; Page 82, "Moms Balance World Cup with Motherhood," *Redbook,* January 20, 2000.
Chapter Nine: Page 88, "Titanic Postcard Helps Save a Life," Access WebWorks, April 20, 1998; Page 94, "Canadian Company Wants Icebergs," Canadian Broadcasting Co. (www.cbc.ca), February 2, 2000.
Chapter Ten: Page 100, "100-Year-Old Woman Becomes U.S. Citizen," *The Seattle Times,* by Christine Claridge, March 22, 1998; Page 106, "Deaf Man Discovers He Can Communicate," *The Denver Post,* by Michael Booth, October 31, 1999.

CONTENTS

Introduction

Inside the News is a high-beginning reading text designed for young adult and adult readers. The book features authentic newspaper articles that have been adapted to the level of this audience. In addition, each high-interest reading has been selected for its positive, "good news" focus.

The newspaper theme is emphasized throughout the text with photos that originally accompanied the news stories and with reading and writing exercises that explore facets of a daily newspaper. A "Wrap Up" conclusion to each chapter encourages students to discuss aspects of the chapter's theme.

Inside the News is based on several assumptions about the reading process:

1) *Readers understand what they are reading by relating it to their background knowledge about a subject and, when necessary, adapting what they know to accommodate the new information they have gained from the reading.*

2) *Making predictions about a reading opens the door to active engagement with the text.* These assumptions are realized in "Before You Read," the introductory exercise in each chapter. These exercises utilize prior knowledge and encourage students to speculate about the reading based on the photo and the headline.

3) *Having a purpose for reading increases reading comprehension.* "After You Read" helps students check their understanding and confirm the answers which they gave in "Before You Read." A focus on the newspaper reporter's five W's and H (*who, what, when, where, why,* and *how*) causes readers to seek out the important elements of each story. This section of each chapter includes a variety of vocabulary and cloze exercises.

4) *Readers can understand grammatical structures in the context of a reading that they cannot analyze or produce.* Although the vocabulary and structures in *Inside the News* are carefully controlled to accommodate the beginning reader, the readings remain lively and natural, with varying tenses where appropriate.

5) *Vocabulary is developed through use of context clues while reading and through use of target words in other contexts.* "Find the Meaning" exercises that follow each reading use this approach.

6) *Even beginning readers benefit from learning to use reading strategies.* "Improve Your Reading" emphasizes sound strategies that grow out of the reading focus in each chapter.

7) *Practice is essential for the beginning reader.* It is the best means to attaining fluency and developing comprehension. "Extra! Extra Reading!" is a second reading that gives additional practice.

8) *Low-level readers can have high-level thinking skills.* Thought-provoking comprehension questions as well as wrap-up discussion questions encourage the reader to make inferences and express opinions on the content of the chapter.

The assumptions of sound reading theory, authentic high-interest newspaper stories, and the all-encompassing newspaper theme are what make *Inside the News* unique.

Chapter 1

GROUP HELPS OTHERS TO BUILD HOUSES

BEFORE YOU READ

▶ **Use what you know.** Talk about these questions with your classmates.

1. Do most people in your hometown live in apartments or in houses?
2. What does a family do when they want to get a house?
3. Who helps them to buy or build a home?
4. What can poor people do when they need a house?

▶ **Make a guess.** Look at the pictures and think about these questions.

1. How many people are there?
2. What is the man in the picture on the right doing?
3. What things does he need to do the job?
4. Is it difficult to build a house?

▶ **Find the answers.** Look at the title. When you read the story, try to answer these questions.

1. What is the name of the group?
2. Who do they help?
3. How do they help them?

READING

Group Helps Others to Build Houses

1   TEPETITAN, EL SALVADOR—Evinor Mira is only sixteen years old, but he is working as hard as an **adult** man to help his family get a good house. Evinor lives with his mother and his little brother and sister in Tepetitan, El Salvador. His father is **dead**, and the family is very **poor**. Their house is a **tiny** shack of mud and sticks, so Evinor is working with an **organization** called Habitat for Humanity to build a new home.

2   Habitat for Humanity helps people who need houses but do not have much money. Habitat volunteers help to build the houses, but the families do a lot of the work themselves. Each family buys the house through affordable monthly payments. Their payments help build more houses because banks can then **lend** money to other families. Habitat for Humanity **volunteers** help to build the house, but the families must do a lot of the work themselves.

3   Every morning, Evinor begins at 7:00. He and the volunteer workers from Habitat carry boards, pound nails, and pour concrete all day, six days a week. The other workers can go home and rest at 4:00 p.m., but Evinor's day isn't **over**. He rides a bus for forty minutes to go to school in another town. He is in high school and **attends** classes for four hours every evening. At 9:00 p.m. he has to walk two and a half hours to get home because there aren't any buses so late at night. Around 11:30 p.m. he arrives home and does his homework. On Sundays, Evinor works with the Habitat organization to help other families get houses, too.

4   Evinor does not have the easy life of many teenagers, but he doesn't mind working so hard. He is **proud** that he can help his own family and others in his community to have better lives.

AFTER YOU READ

▶ Check your understanding.

Write *true* or *false* for each of these statements.

_____   1. Evinor lives with his mother and father.

_____   2. Evinor's mother does not have enough money to buy a big, beautiful house.

_____ 3. Evinor is building his family's new house all by himself.

_____ 4. Building a house takes a lot of hard work.

_____ 5. Habitat for Humanity gives a free house to anyone who wants one.

Circle the letter of the best answer.

1. Tepetitan is in
   a. El Salvador.   b. Mexico   c. the United States

2. Habitat for Humanity helps poor people to
   a. buy food.   b. get good houses.   c. go to school.

3. The volunteers work on the houses because
   a. they want to help other people.
   b. they can make a lot of money.
   c. they are too lazy to work at another job.

4. Evinor goes to school in the evening because
   a. he works on the house in the daytime.
   b. his mother drives him to school when she finishes work.
   c. it is too hot to go to school in the daytime.

5. Evinor does his homework
   a. on the bus.
   b. before school in the morning.
   c. after he goes home at night.

Write answers to these questions.

1. How old is Evinor?

   _____

2. Where does he live?

   _____

3. Why is he working so hard to build a house?

   _____

4. Is Evinor sad because he doesn't have much free time?

_____

5. Why does Evinor work with the Habitat organization on Sundays?

_____

Think about these questions. If you cannot find the answers in the reading, tell what you think is probably true.

6. Is there a high school in Evinor's village? Explain your answer.

_____

7. Do you think that Tepetitan is a small village or a large city? Why?

_____

8. How does Evinor's mother probably feel about what Evinor is doing?

_____

FIND THE MEANING

▶ **Vocabulary.** Look at the story again. What do you think these words mean? Match each word with the best meaning.

_____ 1. adult (adj.)	a.	finished
_____ 2. dead (adj.)	b.	go to
_____ 3. poor (adj.)	c.	feeling good about what you do
_____ 4. tiny (adj.)	d.	give to someone for a time
_____ 5. organization (n.)	e.	grown up
_____ 6. lend (v.)	f.	very small
_____ 7. volunteer (n.)	g.	not living
_____ 8. over (adj.)	h.	having little money
_____ 9. attend (v.)	i.	person who works without pay
_____ 10. proud (adj.)	j.	group of people working together

▶ **Cloze.** Circle the best word for each space.

My name is Ron. I am a teacher at Mapleton High School, but on Saturdays I am a (volunteer, employee, student) for Habitat for Humanity. This is (a bank, a store, an organization) that helps people who need houses. If they are too (rich, poor, old) to buy a house, Habitat will (lend, give, pay) money to them to build a house, but they must pay the money back to the organization. They can pay a little every month.

The people who need the house also have to work to build it, but they don't have to do it alone. There are always a few helpers. Most of the volunteers who work on the houses are (adults, children, girls), but many young people also come to help. Sometimes I ask a few students who (attend, leave, work at) Mapleton High School to work with me. They are very tired when the day is (beginning, new, over), but they are (sad, proud, afraid) of their work. I think that they learn some important lessons. They learn how to build houses and how to help others.

IMPROVE YOUR READING

▶ **Connecting words.**

We can join two simple sentences with a connecting word to make a longer sentence.

Example: His father is dead. The family is very poor.
              His father is dead, and the family is very poor.

Find some more examples of the following connecting words in the story about Evinor.

 and   *but*   *because*   *so*

1. Which connecting word joins two similar ideas?
2. Which connecting word joins two different ideas?
3. Which connecting word comes before a reason for something (the part of the sentence that tells why)?
4. Which connecting word comes before a result?

Choose the best word to join each of the following sentences.

1. Volunteers work very hard, (because, so, but) they do not receive any money for their work.
2. Evinor takes the bus to another town (but, because) he goes to school there.
3. Habitat for Humanity lends families money, (and, so, because) it sends volunteers to help the family.
4. Building a house is very hard work, (because, so, but) the workers are very tired at the end of the day.
5. Many people want to be Habitat volunteers (and, but, because) they like to help other people.
6. Usually the workers are adults, (so, because, but) there are some teenagers who help too.
7. Evinor works on the house, (and, because, so) he goes to school in the evening.
8. He is proud (because, so, but) he is helping his family.

EXTRA! EXTRA READING!

Frenchman's Dream Apartment Turns into Nightmare

ARLES, FRANCE—André Raffay has a problem. He needs a nice, large apartment in the city of Arles, but he doesn't have enough money to buy one. Every morning André sits in his neighborhood cafe and reads the apartment ads in the newspaper. He draws a circle around each ad for an apartment that looks good. Then he goes to the telephone to call the owner.

"Hello. I'm interested in the apartment near the park that is in today's paper," he says. "How much is it?" When he hears the answer, he says, "Oh, my goodness! That's too much!" The same thing happens every day.

One morning André sees a friend in the cafe. He tells him about his problem. "I have a good idea, André. I know a 90-year-old woman who has a beautiful apartment. You can pay her something every month until she dies. Then you can move into the apartment. It will be yours!"

André is excited. He thinks to himself, "How much longer can such an old lady live? We can probably have the apartment in a couple of years." He and his wife, Marie, go to visit Mrs. Calment. The apartment is just what they want. It is large and sunny, and it is near the center of town. It even has a view of the park.

André tells Mrs. Calment, "We will pay you $500 a month, and you can stay here for the rest of your life." She is very happy. She says, "I really want to stay here. This is my home. Now I don't have to move to my niece's house in the country."

They sign a contract that says that André and his wife will pay Mrs. Calment $500 every month. When she dies, the apartment will belong to André and his wife.

More than thirty years go by. Jeanne Calment is still alive. She is 121 years old, the oldest person in the world. Poor André isn't alive anymore, but his widow still sends Mrs. Calment $500 every month. Their dream apartment is a nightmare.

▶ Comprehension questions.

1. What does André want at the beginning of the story?
2. Why is it difficult to find an apartment?
3. Who does his friend want him to talk to?
4. How old is Mrs. Calment when André and his wife first meet her?
5. Why do André and his wife like the apartment?
6. How much will they pay the old lady every month?
7. Does Mrs. Calment want to stay in her apartment, or does she want to move out?
8. How old is Mrs. Calment at the end of the story?
9. What is a nightmare? Why is the apartment a nightmare for André's wife?

INSIDE THE NEWSPAPER

▶ Classified ads.

Classified ads, or classifieds, are short advertisements that help you to buy or sell something or to find a job or an apartment. The cost of a classified ad depends on the number of words, so the ads are usually very short.

Read each ad and match it with the person who might answer it.

a. Joe wants a bicycle to ride to school.
b. Tod and Chen need an apartment near the college. They each can pay $450 a month.
c. Lee's older brother just gave him some old photographs of famous singers.
d. Maria is looking for a job. She has worked for five years in an office in New York.
e. Jackie is a teenager who needs money for new clothes.
f. Mark is going away to college in another state, and he needs a car to drive.

For Sale: 1999 Toyota Celica, white, two-door, radio, CD player, stick shift. Troy 886-6219.

_____ 1.

For Rent: 2-bedroom apartment in College Park, $900/month. Heat, electricity included. Jim 602-3333.

_____ 2.

For Sale: Red mountain bike, almost new, $80. Mary, 898-0765.

_____ 3.

Help Wanted: Secretary with good computer skills for part-time job in oil company. Ted James, 667-1234.

_____ 4.

Help Wanted: Baby-sitter for 7-year-old boy, 3-5 p.m. Monday-Friday. Mrs. Adams, 979-0765.

_____ 5.

Wanted to Buy: Photos of Elvis Presley. Will pay $$$$. Ali, 834-1254.

_____ 6.

Now look at the want ads from an actual newspaper. Choose two that you are interested in. With a partner, discuss the answers to these questions. Then tell the class about the ads that you read.

1. What is the general classification for this ad (cars for sale, help wanted, apartments for rent, etc.)?
2. What is the specific ad for (a Honda Accord, a job as a bank teller, a two-bedroom apartment, etc.)?
3. Are there any abbreviations in the ad (low mi., 2 bdrm.)? What do you think they mean?
4. How can you get more information about the thing in the ad? Is there an address, a telephone number, or a postal box number?

WRITE ALL ABOUT IT

Try writing one of these ads in as few words as you can. Look at the ads above as examples.

1. Wanted to Rent: Vacation House
   Tell what kind of house you're looking for, when, where, and how much you can pay.
2. For Sale: Car
   You need to sell your car for as much money as possible. Describe the make, year, model, color and any extras. Tell how much money you are selling it for.
3. For Sale: Furniture
   You are a student who is returning home to your country. You want to sell all the furniture in your one-bedroom apartment.

WRAP UP

Prepare to talk to your classmates or write about one of these topics.

1. Describe your dream home. Where is it? How big is it? What does it look like?
2. Habitat for Humanity helps people get houses. What are some other ways that we can help people who do not have much money?
3. How does a person or a family usually find a house or an apartment in your home country? Tell about the steps that they follow.

Chapter 2

FAST PIGEONS HELP PHOTOGRAPHER

BEFORE YOU READ

▶ **Use what you know.** Talk about these questions with your classmates.

1. How can animals help people? What are some jobs that they can do for people?
2. What is a pigeon? Where can you see pigeons? What can they do for people?
3. What are some kinds of water sports? Which water sports do you like?
4. Would you like to take a rafting trip on a river? Why or why not?
5. What does a photographer do? Do you think that a photographer has an interesting job?

▶ **Make a guess.** Look at the picture on page 11and answer these questions.

1. What can you see in the picture?
2. What are the people doing?
3. Where are they?
4. Are they having a good time?

▶ **Find the answers.** Now read the story. Think about these questions.

1. Who is Bill Jones?
2. What does he take photos of?
3. Where does Bill put the film after he takes pictures?
4. How does Bill get the film back to the store?
5. When can the people on the raft see the photographs?
6. Write one question that you have about the story.

_____ ?

READING

Fast Pigeons Help Photographer

1   FORT COLLINS, COLORADO—Bill Jones, a Colorado **photographer** who takes pictures of river rafters, has a good idea. He uses **pigeons** to make his photography business better and faster.

2   Bill stands on rocks high above the Poudre River. He has several cameras and a small cage with a pigeon in it. As he looks down at the river, he sees a rubber **raft moving rapidly** toward him. In the boat are seven rafters and a **guide**. They are shouting as the raft goes up and over the white water. It looks like the raft is going to hit a big rock in the middle of the river. "Watch out!" Bill says to himself. "Use your paddles to go around the rock." Each rafter paddles hard, and the raft just misses the rock. What an **exciting** trip!

3   Bill gets his camera ready. He knows that the people in the raft will want to buy photos as soon as they finish their river trip. He takes twelve fast photos of the raft as it goes up and over the white water below him. He takes the film out of the camera. How can he quickly get the film to his store, which is twenty miles down the mountain road?

4   Bill takes a gray-and-white pigeon out of the little cage. He puts the film from the camera into a very small **backpack** on the back of the bird. "O.K., Petie. Fly as fast as you can," Bill says. The pigeon knows how to fly very fast to the store, which is its home.

5   When the pigeon gets there, Bill's **assistant**, David Moore, takes the film from the bird's back. He uses the film to make photographs of the people on the river. After the rafters finish the river trip, they are wet and tired, but they are happy. They hurry to Bill's store. "I can't wait to see the photos of our raft going over the white water," one of the rafters says. "I want to buy all the photos to show to my friends."

6   The rafters buy many photos. They also ask many questions about the pigeons. "How fast do your pigeons fly?" one rafter asks. "They fly about one mile (1.6 km.) a minute," Bill says, "so it takes them about twenty minutes to fly from the river to the store."

7   Another rafter laughs and asks, "How much do you pay the pigeons to help you?" Bill answers, "We give them a warm place to live and lots of food to eat. That's all they want."

AFTER YOU READ

▶ Check your understanding.

Write *true* or *false* for each of these sentences. Rewrite each false sentence correctly.

Example: _false_   Bill lives and works in California.
                          Bill lives and works in Colorado.

_____   1. Bill is a river guide.

_____

_____   2. Bill is in the raft with the rafters.

_____

_____   3. Bill is taking pictures of the people in the raft.

_____

_____   4. The pigeon knows how to return to the store.

_____

_____   5. David works in the store.

_____

Circle the letter of the best answer.

1. A rafter is
   a. a kind of bird.
   b. a person who uses a raft.
   c. a person who takes photographs.

2. Bill uses the pigeon because
   a. it is very cheap.
   b. it is very fast.
   c. it can swim in the river.

3. David's job is
   a. helping people on the rafts.
   b. making pictures.
   c. selling pigeons.

4. The pigeon flies to the store because
   a. it wants to help Bill.
   b. it can hear David calling it.
   c. the store is its home.

5. The people on the raft trip want to
   a. buy the pictures of themselves on the raft.
   b. buy some pictures of the pigeons.
   c. buy their own raft.

Write answers to these questions.

1. What is Bill's job?

   _____

2. Who is Bill's assistant?

   _____

3. What can the pigeons do?

   _____

4. What are the people on the river doing?

   _____

5. Where can they buy pictures of their rafting trip?

   _____

6. Why do Bill and David use the pigeons?

   _____

FIND THE MEANING

▶ **Vocabulary.** Look at the story again. What do you think these words mean? Try to guess the meaning from the information in the story. Match each word with the best meaning.

_____ 1. cage	a. a kind of boat
_____ 2. moving	b. a bag you carry on your back
_____ 3. raft	c. a person who takes pictures
_____ 4. rapidly	d. a kind of box where an animal lives
_____ 5. guide	e. a kind of bird
_____ 6. photographer	f. going from one place to another
_____ 7. exciting	g. a person who leads or shows the way
_____ 8. pigeon	h. quickly
_____ 9. backpack	I. helper
_____ 10. assistant	j. interesting and fun

▶ **Cloze.** **Fill in each blank with the correct vocabulary word from the story.**

photographs	quickly	raft	miles
photographer	moves	trip	~~mountains~~

Dear Carlos,

Tony and I are having a great vacation here in Colorado. The *mountains*
are wonderful. The scenery is beautiful, and there are many things to do. Of course,
you can camp, hike, and fish, but the best thing is going down a river on a
_____ . In the small mountain town there is a company that takes
you on the trip. First, you ride in their car for about twenty _____ to
a special place on the river. Then you put the raft in the water and get in. A guide
from the company comes with you to help you. He tells you what to do. The water
_____ very fast, and the raft moves very _____ . It is
a little scary, but it is a lot of fun. There is a _____ who stands near
the river and takes pictures. How do you think he gets the film to the store? He
sends it on the back of a pigeon! Really! He says it is very fast, and the
_____ are ready when you finish your _____ . We
will show you ours when we get home. See you soon! Say hi to everyone.

Yours,

Nick

IMPROVE YOUR READING

▶ **Suffixes.**

A suffix is a syllable added at the end of a word. A suffix often changes the part of
speech of a word and sometimes has a meaning. Two examples of suffixes in the story
are *-er* and *-ly*.

The suffix *-er* is used to mean *a person who* _____ .

Examples from the story:

photograph   +   *-er*   =   photograph<u>er</u>

raft   +   *-er*   =   raft<u>er</u>

A *rafter* is a person who rides on a raft.

What is a photographer?

A *photographer* is a person who _____ .

Other common examples:

teach   →   teach<u>er</u>
write   →   writ<u>er</u>
help   →   help<u>er</u>

Add *-er* to each of these words to make a new word that means *a person who* _____ .

1. work _____

2. own _____

3. play _____

4. drive _____

Write some more examples.

5. _____

6. _____

7. _____

8. _____

9. _____

10. _____

The suffix *-ly* changes an adjective to an adverb. An adverb tells <u>how</u> we do something.

Examples from the story:

adjective	adverb
rapid	rapid<u>ly</u>
quick	quick<u>ly</u>

The word *quickly* tells us how Bill gets the film to the store.

The word *rapidly* tells us how _____ .

Other common examples:

adjective		adverb
correct	→	correct<u>ly</u>
slow	→	slow<u>ly</u>
loud	→	loud<u>ly</u>
soft	→	soft<u>ly</u>

Fill in each blank with the adverb (-*ly*) form of the word.

1. My teacher writes _____*neatly*_____ (neat).

2. Mika speaks _____ (polite) to her parents.

3. Luis plays the guitar _____ (beautiful).

4. The mother picks up her baby _____ (careful).

5. The boys entered the room _____ (silent).

EXTRA! EXTRA READING!

Dog Is Girl's Bridge to the World

DENVER, COLORADO—They're best friends. They go to school together every day. They hang out at the shopping mall on weekends. Both of them have hair the color of honey, but one has big blue eyes and the other deep brown eyes.

One of the friends, Jenny Siegle, is in a wheelchair. The other, Augie, is an amazing dog who helps Jenny. Jenny, who is 14 years old, is a quadriplegic, which means she cannot use her arms or legs. Augie, a golden retriever, is a Freedom Service dog who is Jenny's arms and legs.

How does Augie do this? In school, he picks up the pencil or notebook that Jenny drops. Jenny is also training Augie to pull off her jacket so Jenny doesn't have to ask anyone for help.

At home, Augie brings her the TV listings. He even helps clean Jenny's room. When Jenny asks him, Augie goes to get her parents or sister. Augie also carries his food dish back to Jenny so she can fill it with dog food. Then Augie puts it back neatly in its place.

At the mall, Augie wears a backpack that tells everyone he is a Freedom Service dog. When Jenny wants to buy things, Augie carries them to the counter. He gives the cashier Jenny's wallet and waits for the change.

P. J. Roche, a dog trainer who started Freedom Service Dogs, says, "These dogs are a social bridge. Kids who don't know Jenny come up to talk to her because she's got a dog." Augie is truly Jenny's best friend and helper and her bridge to the world.

▶ Comprehension questions.

1. Who is Augie? Describe him.
2. Who is Jenny? Describe her.
3. Why does Augie help Jenny?
4. What things does Augie do to help Jenny at school?
5. What things does Augie do to help Jenny at home?
6. What does Augie do to help Jenny at the mall?
7. Augie is Jenny's bridge to the world. What does this mean?
8. The story about the pigeon is about an animal that helps a man do his job. This story is about a dog and a young girl. How are the stories the same?

INSIDE THE NEWSPAPER

▶ Comic strips.

Many people read the comics before any other part of the newspaper. Read the comic strip that follows. Do you think this comic is funny? What makes it funny?

Find another comic from an actual newspaper. Bring it to class, and explain it to your classmates. Tell what is happening in the pictures, what the characters are saying, and why you think it is funny.

WRITE ALL ABOUT IT

In the strip that follows, work with your classmates to make up your own comic. Draw pictures of people or animals. Write the words that they say.

WRAP UP

Prepare to talk to your classmates or write about one of these topics.

1. Find an interesting photo in a newspaper and describe it to your classmates.
2. Tell the class about an interesting animal.
3. Describe your favorite outdoor activity.

 **Inside the NEWS**

Chapter 3

DOLLS TEACH WHAT IT'S LIKE TO BE PARENTS

BEFORE YOU READ

▶ **Use what you know.** Look at the picture. Read the title. Talk about the topic with your classmates. Fill in the map together.

TEENAGERS
HAVING BABIES

Problems   Solutions

for the teenagers	for the babies		control the teenagers	educate the teenagers
have to give up freedom	*often grow up with one parent*		*make them come home early*	

▶ **Make a guess.** Look at the picture on page 21, read the headline below, read the first sentence in each paragraph, and try to answer these questions.

1. What are the teachers at Smoky Hill High School using to teach the students about babies?
2. How long does each student keep the doll?
3. Why do the teachers want the teenagers to learn about babies?
4. Does Kacey think that taking care of a baby doll is a good idea?

▶ **Find the answers.** Now read the story. Think about these questions.

1. What are the teachers in this high school doing to educate the teenagers about having babies?
2. Do the teachers think that this is a good idea?
3. What do the teenagers learn from this experience?
4. Write one question you have about the story.

? _____

READING

Dolls Teach What It's Like to Be Parents

1   AURORA, COLORADO—Baby dolls are teaching **teenagers** what it <u>is like</u> to be parents. At Smoky Hill High School, two boys and 78 girls <u>are caring for</u> the dolls. These dolls are not toys. There is a computer inside each one. The computer <u>keeps track of</u> how well the student <u>takes care of</u> the "baby."

2   The teacher gives each student one baby doll to <u>take care of</u> for 48 hours. If the student **drops** the "baby," it cries. It also cries if the student puts it on its **stomach** or on its left side. It cries again if he or she handles it **roughly**. The doll also cries every 3 1/2 hours, and the "parents" have to put a key into a **hole** in its back. This stops the baby's crying. It is just like having to **feed** a baby every few hours. The students take the dolls **wherever** they go—to school, to work, and to their homes.

3   "My baby cries all the time. I can't study. I can't <u>have fun</u> because she always needs something," one student says.

4   Kim, a 14-year-old girl, thought having a baby would be a lot of fun. "I've always liked to baby-sit, so I thought it would be fun to take care of a baby. But not now! I <u>can't wait</u> **until** this class is finished and I can <u>get away from</u> all the work it takes to care for this doll."

5   Teachers believe this class will make teenagers <u>think twice</u> before getting **pregnant**.

6   "There are a million teen pregnancies a year in the United States," says Lorraine Cortese, who started the program.

7   Many of the girls who become mothers feel that a baby will be something to love. They also want the love that a baby will give to them. They don't know how much work and **trouble** a baby can be. Ms. Cortese believes this program lets teens see how difficult it is to be parents.

8   Kacey Stannard, 15, agrees. She says, "I always wanted a baby, but now I know I'm not ready."

AFTER YOU READ

▶ **Check your understanding.**

Write *true* or *false* for each of these sentences. Write each false sentence correctly.

   Example: *false*   Two girls and 78 boys are caring for the dolls.
                          Two boys and 78 girls are caring for the dolls.

_____   1. The teacher gives each student one baby doll to take care of for 24 hours.

   _____

_____   2. The doll cries every 4 1/2 hours.

   _____

_____   3. These dolls are not toys.

   _____

_____   4. The students take the dolls everywhere.

   _____

_____   5. When the "baby" cries, the student can study.

   _____

Circle the letter of the best answer.

1. There are _____ teen pregnancies a year in the United States.

   a. a million

   b. a thousand

   c. a hundred

2. If the student drops the "baby," it

   a. laughs.

   b. cries.

   c. gets angry.

3. *Teens* means

   a. adults.

   b. babies.

   c. young people from thirteen to nineteen years old.

4. The baby doll cries if the student handles it

   a. roughly.

   b. nicely.

   c. slowly.

5. Some teenage girls think that they want to have babies because

   a. the baby will love them, and they will love the baby.

   b. it is difficult to be a parent.

   c. they like being pregnant.

Write answers to these questions.

1. What is the name of the teenagers' school in this story?

   _____

2. How many students are taking care of the dolls?

   _____

3. What is inside each doll?

   _____

4. What do the students have to do to make the doll stop crying?

   _____

5. Why do the teenagers think that it is not fun to take care of the dolls?

   _____

Give your own opinions about these questions. Explain your answers.

6. Will the teenagers in the story probably get pregnant soon?

   _____

7. Can you think of other ways to teach teenagers how hard it is to take care of a baby?

   _____

8. Most of the teenagers in this story are girls. Should more boys practice taking care of babies?

   _____

FIND THE MEANING

▶ **Vocabulary**. **Look at the story again. What do you think these words mean? Try to guess the meaning from the information in the story. Match each word with the best meaning.**

_____ 1. roughly	a. a small opening
_____ 2. hole	b. expecting a baby
_____ 3. feed	c. in whatever place
_____ 4. pregnant	d. up to the time that
_____ 5. drop	e. a lot of work
_____ 6. teenager	f. not gently
_____ 7. wherever	g. let fall
_____ 8. stomach	h. give food to
_____ 9. until	i. a person thirteen to nineteen years old
_____ 10. trouble	j. middle front part of the body

▶ **Cloze.** Use the following words to fill in the blanks in this conversation between Kim and her friend Jennifer.

backpack	baby	cries	computer	doll
everywhere	fun	leave	pregnant	teach

Jennifer: Hey Kim, what have you got there in your _____ ?

Kim: Oh, this is my baby.

Jennifer: Your baby? You don't have a baby!

Kim: Well, not really, but this _____ is a lot like a baby. I have to carry it

around with me _____ I go for two whole days. It

_____ all the time, and I'm getting so tired of it I could scream.

Jennifer: Where did you get it?

Kim: Ms. Cortese gave one to everyone in the class. It is supposed to

_____ us how hard it is to take care of a _____ .

Jennifer: Well, why don't you just _____ it in your room and forget about

it?

Kim: I can't. For one thing, it cries if I don't take good care of it. Also, it has a

_____ inside, and the teacher can check to see if I'm doing a good

job.

Jennifer: So, are you learning anything from doing this?

Kim: I sure am. I'm learning that babies take a lot of time and work. I love little

kids, but I definitely don't want to get _____ and have one of my

own right now. I'm only fourteen. I want to be able to go out and have

_____ with my friends after school and on weekends.

IMPROVE YOUR READING
....

❱ Idioms.

An idiom is an expression with a special meaning. When you read, it is important to understand the meanings of idioms. Look at the story again. Find the underlined idioms.

Keep track of means to pay attention to what is happening. In this story, the computer understands and records what the students do with the dolls.

Now match each of these other idioms with the best meaning. Which two have the same meaning?

_____	1. be like	a. want to happen
_____	2. care for	b. escape
_____	3. take care of	c. enjoy
_____	4. have fun	d. consider carefully
_____	5. can't wait	e. watch and help
_____	6. get away from	f. be similar to
_____	7. think twice	

Write some other English idioms that you know. Write their meanings.

Idiom	*Meaning*
_____	_____
_____	_____
_____	_____
_____	_____

28

Students Learn at Home in On-line School

ORLANDO, FLORIDA—Is it hard for you to get up early and get ready for classes? Some students at Winter Park High School just roll out of bed in their pajamas and go to class in their own bedrooms. Of course, their teachers and classmates do not see them because all their classwork is on the computer.

The Florida high school, the state's only on-line school, has 250 students who are taking classes at home by computer.

"I'm a lot more comfortable at home," says Luke Levesque, a 16-year-old who is taking a computer class on-line. He thinks the school's computer lab is so noisy that he can't study well. "Home is much better," he says.

Students in this first on-line program take classes in algebra, American government, chemistry, computer, economics, and Web-page design. They also have to go to regular school to attend other classes.

When a student is ready to begin a class, he or she turns on the computer, reads the teacher's instructions, and begins working on the lesson for the day. What happens if a student has a question for the teacher? Or the teacher wants to say something about the work a student is doing? The student and the teacher talk to each other every day through e-mail or by telephone. For example, when Luke opened his daily e-mail from the teacher, it contained her instructions for the day's computer lesson. When he was finished, he e-mailed the work back to her for grading.

Is it easy for students to cheat on tests when they're working at home? The teachers have already thought about this. They make students take their final exams in person in the classroom.

"You see most of the same things on-line that you see in a regular classroom," says teacher Linda Hayes. "You get to know the students on-line. You know the kid who is a real go-getter and the one who isn't."

If this first on-line program goes well, in three years Florida high school students will be able to take all their classes by computer. When that happens, students will be able to get their high school diplomas without having to set foot in a classroom.

▶ Comprehension questions.

1. What is the name of the high school?
2. How many students are taking on-line classes?
3. Why does Luke like the classes he takes at home?
4. How do students talk to each other and the teacher?
5. Is it easy to cheat on tests?
6. What will happen in three years?
7. Would you like to stay at home and go to school on a computer? (What do you think about being a student by computer?)

INSIDE THE NEWSPAPER

❶ Crossword puzzles.

Newspapers often contain crossword puzzles as a fun way to practice vocabulary. Use the clues to complete the puzzle with words from this lesson.

ACROSS

1. Mother or father
3. Schoolwork for students to do at home
4. Another person in your class
7. A test of what you know
9. An enjoyable time
10. A person who teaches in school
11. An electronic machine that stores
13. Teach

DOWN

1. A difficult situation
2. A person who studies at a school or college
5. Something that you study in school
6. A young person between 13 and 19 years old
8. Go to
11. A group of students who learn together
12. A letter that you send by computer

Now find a crossword puzzle in an actual newspaper. With a partner, talk about these questions.

1. Which section of the newspaper is it in?
2. What other things can you find on the same page?
3. How many letters do the longest and shortest words in the puzzle have?
4. When and where can you find the answer to the puzzle?

WRITE ALL ABOUT IT

Write a paragraph that describes the "school of your dreams." Tell about the teacher. Tell what the classrooms look like. What subjects can students study?

WRAP UP

Prepare to talk with your classmates about one of these topics.

1. When you were in high school, did you learn about marriage and babies? Is it good to talk about these things in school?
2. Do you like the idea of using computers at home for school classes? Why or why not?
3. Should boys and men learn how to take care of babies? Why or why not?

Inside the NEWS

Chapter 4

McDONALD'S OPENS RESTAURANT IN NEW DELHI

BEFORE YOU READ

▶ **Use what you know.** Talk about fast-food restaurants with your classmates.
On the map, write a few words that tell about these restaurants.

FAST-FOOD
RESTAURANTS

In the U.S., they are

_____
_____
_____

People like them because

_____
_____
_____

In my country, they are

_____
_____
_____

▶ **Make a guess.** Look at the picture on page 33 and answer these questions.

1. Who do you see in the picture?
2. What is he doing?
3. Where is he?
4. Are there other people in the picture? What are they doing?

▶ **Find the answers.** Now read the story. Think about these questions.

1. Is this McDonald's the same as McDonald's restaurants in the United States?
2. What is the same? What is different?
3. Who comes to eat at the New Delhi McDonald's?
4. Why doesn't this McDonald's serve beef hamburgers?
5. Where does this McDonald's get its food?
6. Write one question that you have about the story.

_____ ?

READING

McDonald's Opens Restaurant in New Delhi

1   NEW DELHI, INDIA—McDonald's is opening its first **restaurant** in New Delhi, India. It is the only McDonald's in the world with no **beef** on the **menu**. You can't find Big Macs here, but there are **mutton** Maharajah Macs. These hamburgers are made from Indian sheep, and the fries are made from Indian potatoes. The soda comes from an Indian bottler.

2   Many old and young people come to the new restaurant. Mr. Sahani, who is 75 years old, says he comes all the way from a town which is 90 miles south of New Delhi. "I like <u>it</u> because McDonald's has not brought things from **overseas**. All the food comes from India."

3   A 19-year-old boy, Pankresh, says, "If the food is good, I don't care where <u>it</u> comes from."

4   A rich Indian man, Vikram Bakshi, owns **half** of the restaurant. The McDonald company owns the other half. Bakshi says the restaurant **serves** mutton because 80 percent of Indians are Hindu. Hindus do not eat beef. <u>They</u> also believe that it is wrong to kill cows.

5   The menu at the New Delhi McDonald's has some other Indian food. For the Indians who do not eat any meat at all, there are **Vegetable** McNuggets. <u>They</u> are made with rice, peas, carrots, red pepper, beans, and spices.

6   McDonald's has 20,000 restaurants in more than 95 countries. <u>It</u> fits its menu to each **culture**. In Thailand, people can eat Samurai Pork Burgers with a sweet **sauce** on top. In Japan they can try a burger topped with a fried egg.

AFTER YOU READ

▶ **Check your understanding.**

Write *true* or *false* for each of these sentences. Write each false sentence correctly.

Example: _*false*_   This is the second McDonald's restaurant in New Delhi, India.
                    This is the first McDonald's restaurant in New Delhi, India.

_____   1. Most McDonald's restaurants in the world make the hamburgers from beef.

_____

_____   2. You can order fries at the New Delhi McDonald's.

_____

_____   3. Only young people like to eat at McDonald's in India.

_____

_____   4. Pankresh eats at McDonald's because the food is cheap.

_____

_____   5. All the people in India are Hindu.

_____

Circle the letter of the best answer.

1. Mr. Bakshi
   a. works as a waiter in this McDonald's.
   b. owns 50 percent of the restaurant.
   c. comes to the restaurant to eat.

2. The food at the New Delhi McDonald's comes from
   a. the United States.
   b. many different countries.
   c. India.

3. The McNuggets at this McDonald's are made from
   a. chicken.
   b. mutton.
   c. vegetables.

4. Many Indians do not eat beef because
   a. they don't like the taste of beef.
   b. Hindus believe it is bad to kill cows.
   c. beef is very expensive in India.

5. McDonald's restaurants serve
   a. only American food.
   b. only all-beef hamburgers.
   c. food that the people in each different country like.

Complete the questions for these answers.

Example: *Where is the only McDonald's in the world with no beef?*
The only McDonald's in the world with no beef is in New Delhi.

1. What kind of _____ do they use at the McDonald's in New Delhi ?
   They use mutton in the burgers at McDonald's in New Delhi.

2. Where does _____ come from?
   Mr. Sahani comes from a town which is 90 miles south of New Delhi.

3. Who is _____ ?
   Vikram Bakshi is the man who owns half of the New Delhi McDonald's.

4. Why do they make _____ ?
    They make the burgers from mutton because Hindus do not eat beef.

5. How many _____ does McDonald's have?
    McDonald's has 20,000 restaurants.

Now write five more questions to ask your classmates about the story.

1. _____ ?

2. _____ ?

3. _____ ?

4. _____ ?

5. _____ ?

FIND THE MEANING

▶ **Vocabulary.** Look at the story again. Try to guess what these words mean. Match each word with the best definition.

_____ 1. sauce	a. meat from a cow
_____ 2. beef	b. meat from a sheep
_____ 3. menu	c. liquid to make food taste good
_____ 4. restaurant	d. list of food in a restaurant
_____ 5. mutton	e. a place to buy and eat meals
_____ 6. overseas	f. a plant that we eat
_____ 7. half	g. give someone food or drink
_____ 8. vegetable	h. 50 percent
_____ 9. culture	i. how people in a country live
_____ 10. serve	j. on a different continent

▶ **Cloze.** Fill in each blank with the correct vocabulary word from the story.

restaurants	mutton	serve	sauce	beef
French fries	menus	soda	beans	

Nutrition News

Many people think that it is not good for their health to eat a lot of meat, so they try not to eat too much _____ or _____ . They want information about other things that they can eat. Of course, it is not good to eat a lot of fried food like _____ , and it isn't good for you to drink a lot of _____ . There are some non-meat foods that are delicious and healthful. Many _____ now have some of these foods on their _____ . For example, they sometimes _____ burgers that they make from vegetables, not from beef. At home you can make some interesting dishes without meat, too. You can cook _____ and rice, or you can put _____ on vegetables to make them taste good. These kinds of foods are good for your health, and they are not expensive.

IMPROVE YOUR READING

▶ **Pronouns.**

Pronouns are words that replace nouns in sentences. When you read, it is important to understand which noun the pronoun is talking about. For example, look at the second sentence of the story.

It is the only McDonald's in the world with no beef on the menu.
it = the first McDonald's in New Delhi

Find these other sentences in the story. Circle the letter of the noun that the underlined pronoun refers to.

1. I like <u>it</u> because McDonald's has not brought things from overseas.

   a. the restaurant   b. a town   c. New Delhi

2. If the food is good, I don't care where <u>it</u> comes from.

   a. a boy   b. the food   c. the restaurant

3. <u>They</u> also believe that it is wrong to kill cows.

   a. the men who own McDonald's

   b. cows

   c. Hindus

4. <u>They</u> are made with rice, peas, carrots, red peppers, beans, and spices.

   a. Vegetable McNuggets

   b. hamburgers

   c. the menu

5. <u>It</u> fits its menu to each culture.

   a. McDonald's   b. countries   c. Indians

EXTRA! EXTRA READING!

Hot Climates and Hot Food Go Together

NEW YORK, NEW YORK—Why do you think people who live in some hot countries eat very spicy food? Is it because the spices make the food taste better? Is it just because their parents and grandparents and great-grandparents liked hot food, or is there some connection between spices and healthy food?

Researchers from Cornell University think that it is because spice plants contain some important chemicals. These chemicals can kill bacteria which spoil food. "Most common spices like garlic, onion, and hot peppers can kill 75 to 100 percent of the bacteria in food," explains one of the biologists. The bacteria grow more easily and spoil food more quickly at higher temperatures. For this reason, it is more difficult to keep food from spoiling in hot climates.

To begin this study, the researchers studied cookbooks from 36 countries to learn how often the traditional recipes called for spices. They learned that more spices were used in the hot countries. For example, Mexican cooks use hot peppers. In the Arab Gulf, they use cumin, garlic, and cardamom. India is famous for its spicy curries, which call for curry powder, turmeric, and cardamom.

Researchers also found that people in colder countries use very few of the spices that cooks use in warmer parts of the world. Canadian cooks, for example, don't use hot peppers very often. Danish, Swedish, and Norwegian food is very mild because it has few spices.

Do you like your food spicy or mild? Your answer probably tells something about the country you come from. If you like spicy food, it is possible that hundreds of years ago, when there were no refrigerators, people in your country started using spices to keep the food from spoiling. The traditional spicy dishes helped those people to live longer, healthier lives. Today, in a time of refrigerators and freezers, the spices just make the food taste good.

▶ Comprehension questions.

1. How do the chemicals in spices keep food from spoiling?
2. What did the researchers do to learn about the spices that people use in different countries?
3. Why does food spoil more quickly in hot climates?
4. What is an example of a cold country where people do not eat spicy food?
5. What is an example of a hot country where they cook with a lot of spices?
6. Do most people in your country like spicy food?

INSIDE THE NEWSPAPER

▶ Restaurant ads.

Read the four restaurant ads. Answer the questions.

1. What is the name of the Chinese restaurant?

_____

2. The Egg Place serves breakfast. What is a special food they want you to buy?

_____

3. Where is Simply Sushi?

_____

4. Which restaurant gives you 25 % off your breakfast? If your meal is $4, how much do you pay?

_____

5. Where can you go for pizza and Italian food? How much is their dinner special?

_____

The
Egg
Place
Come join us for
breakfast or lunch
25% OFF
from 6-8 a.m.
Try our cinnamon rolls!
I-225 and
Parker Rd

Simply
Sushi

Your friendly
neighborhood
sushi bar and
restaurant

1022 West Fifth St.

Lotus
Chinese

Lunch
Special $4.95

On
Sherman St.
and 14th

Tony's Pizza
Dinner Special: $7.50
Pasta with garlic,
spinach, and olives (includes soup and salad bar)
Outdoor Tables • Italian Wine
Open every day from 12 noon to 10 p.m.
305 North St. • 555-8999

Now look at restaurant ads in an actual newspaper. Answer these questions.

1. What kind of food does the restaurant serve?
2. Where is the restaurant?
3. What days and what hours is it open?
4. How much does a meal at the restaurant cost?

WRITE ALL ABOUT IT

Pretend that you are the owner of a restaurant. Make a newspaper advertisement for your restaurant. Include the name of the restaurant, the kind of food, the location of the restaurant, and the hours it is open.

WRAP UP

Talk with your classmates or write about one of these topics.

1. Describe your favorite restaurant. Where is it? What do you see there? What do you hear? What do you smell? Why do you like the food?
2. What are some foods in your country that people in other countries do not eat?
3. Describe a typical meal with your family.

Chapter 5

THIS ROBOT LOVES PEOPLE

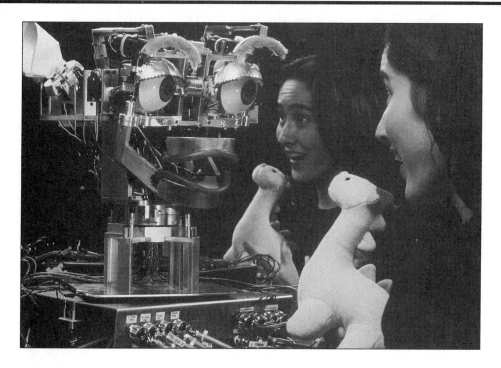

BEFORE YOU READ

▶ **Use what you know.** Freewriting: Write for three minutes nonstop about robots. Do not worry about organization, grammar, or spelling. Just write everything you can think of. When you finish, share your ideas with your classmates. What do robots look like? How can we use them? Make a list of vocabulary words that you use in your discussion.

▶ **Make a guess.** Look at the title and the picture and answer these questions.

1. In what ways does this robot look like a human being?
2. What are some ways that people show love for each other?
3. How do you think a robot can love a person?

▶ **Find the answers.** Think about these questions as you read the story.

1. Who made this robot?
2. What does it look like?
3. What does the robot do when the researcher comes in, sits down, and talks to it?
4. How do the parts of the robot move?
5. In what way is this robot different from most other robots?

This Robot Loves People

1   CAMBRIDGE, MASSACHUSETTS — If you walk by the **workbench** in Cynthia Breazeal's **laboratory**, you'll look twice! There on the workbench is a large piece of aluminum filled with computer chips and electric motors. It looks like a human head, and it looks lonely. Its big, red, **rubber** lips are turned down in a frown. Its **fuzzy** eyebrows are heavy. Its curly pink ears are turned down, and its big blue eyes are looking around the room, **searching** for someone.

2   Breazeal is a researcher at the Artificial Intelligence Lab at the Massachusetts Institute of Technology. When she comes into the lab, she sits down in front of the sad little robot that she made. Right away, the robot, whose name is Kismet, turns **toward** her. Breazeal smiles and the robot's eyebrows go straight up. Kismet looks interested. Then Kismet **wiggles** its ears up and down to greet her. Kismet smiles because it is happy. Next Breazeal talks baby talk to the robot, just like a new mother. That makes Kismet pay attention. It smiles and watches. Then Breazeal sways back and forth in front of Kismet. Kismet doesn't like that at all. It looks **annoyed**. Kismet turns up a lip, raises one eyebrow and lowers the other. The message is clear: Stop this nonsense!

3   Breazeal can keep Kismet happy by paying attention to the robot just like a mother keeps a baby happy. She can pick up a toy dinosaur and begin playing with Kismet. Kismet likes that. But sometimes the robot becomes tired, closes its eyes, and goes to sleep.

4   Is Kismet just a toy that the researchers made to act like this? The answer is "no." Kismet is **reacting** to what it "sees." A color CCD camera is set into each eye. Small motors move the eyebrows, lips, mouth, and ears. Breazeal also wrote special software for Kismet. She calls the software "drives" and "emotions." Drives are the need for people, the need to have things to watch and play with, and the need to sleep. The emotions are happiness, anger, calm, fear, interest, sadness, and so on. You don't always know what Kismet will do because it reacts to what it "sees." The researcher

hopes to **program** the robot to need learning. Learning will make the robot happy. As it begins to learn, it will grow from a "baby" to a "child."

5   Breazeal says that her work is still research, but she believes that Kismet is a step into the future. "This is the kind of robot that goes beyond something that just takes out the trash or delivers medicines in a hospital," she says. If Breazeal has her wish, robots will be more than machines. They may even be our friends.

AFTER YOU READ

▶ Check your understanding.

Write *true* or *false* for each of these sentences. If you think a statement is false, explain why you think so.

_____   1. The big piece of aluminum filled with motors and computer chips is a robot.

_____

_____   2. Cynthia Breazeal is a high school student.

_____

_____   3. Kismet can walk around and take out the trash.

_____

_____   4. Human beings have drives and emotions, but most robots do not.

_____

_____   5. This robot is different from a human child because it will never be able to learn.

_____

Complete the statements.

Example: Ms. Breazeal is a researcher at *the Massachusetts Institute of Technology*.

1. When there is nobody working in the lab, the robot feels _____ .

2. When Kismet greets Breazeal, it _____ .

3. When the robot is happy, it _____ .

4. When the robot is a little angry, it _____ .

5. When Kismet gets angry, it _____ .

Write answers to these questions.

1. What is Kismet?

   _____

2. What is Kismet made of?

   _____

3. Who is Cynthia Breazeal?

   _____

4. Where does she work?

   _____

5. What does Kismet do when people look at it and talk to it?

   _____

6. Is Kismet just a toy? Why not?

   _____

7. What emotions does Kismet show?

   _____

8. What drives does Kismet have?

   _____

9. What does Ms. Breazeal hope to do in the future?

   _____

10. What can robots become in the future if Ms. Breazeal has her wish?

    _____

FIND THE MEANING

▶ **Vocabulary.** Match each word with the best meaning.

_____ 1. workbench (n.)   a. give instructions to a computer

_____ 2. laboratory (n.)   b. look for someone or something

_____ 3. rubber (n.)   c. a tough, stretchy material used to make tires

_____ 4. fuzzy (adj.)   d. a room where scientists perform experiments

_____ 5. search (v.)   e. made of soft, fluffy hair

_____ 6. toward (prep.)   f. a long table where someone works

_____ 7. wiggle (v.)   g. in the direction of

_____ 8. annoyed (adj.)   h. move with quick, short movements

_____ 9. react (v.)   i. a little bit angry

_____ 10. program (v.)   j. respond; do something because of
                                       something else

▶ **Cloze.** Fill in each blank with the correct vocabulary word from the story.

annoyed (adj.)	program (v.)	researcher (n.)	person (n.)	react (v.)
eyebrows (n.)	motors (n.)	experiment (n.)	need (v.)	real (v.)

Imagine that Ms. Breazeal is visiting her nephew's class. She is telling them about her job.

"I have a very interesting job. I'm a _____ at MIT. That means I work with other scientists, and we do experiments. Here's a picture of my favorite _____ . This is Kismet. It looks a little like a _____ . You can see that it has eyes, _____ , and a mouth. I made it out of aluminum. I put small _____ in it to make the parts move. Then I put in computer chips because I wanted to _____ it. I programmed it to _____ like a person when it sees something. When I sit down and talk to it, it acts like a baby. It smiles because it is happy to see me. It likes to have me play with it, but it gets _____ sometimes, too. It even gets tired and goes to sleep. However, it doesn't _____ to eat, it can't cry, and it never needs clean diapers. I don't want it to act too much like a _____ baby!

IMPROVE YOUR READING

▶ Compound words.

Compound words are words that we make by putting two shorter words together. When you read, you can understand the meaning of many compound words by looking at the meaning of each part. For example, in this chapter, you read the word workbench. You know that work is a job that someone does, and you know that a bench is a long table, so you can understand that a workbench is a long table where someone does his/her job.

Write the meaning of each smaller word. Then guess the meaning of each of these compound words from the readings in this book. Try not to use your dictionary.

    Example: class = _a group of people who go to school together_

                  mate = _a friend or partner_

                  classmate = _a person in the same class at school_

1. teen = _____

    age = _____

    teenage = _____

2. news = _____

    paper = _____

    newspaper = _____

3. home = _____

    work = _____

    homework = _____

4. back = _____

    pack = _____

    backpack = _____

5. week = _____

   end = _____

   weekend = _____

6. wheel = _____

   chair = _____

   wheelchair = _____

7. note = _____

   book = _____

   notebook = _____

8. bed = _____

   room = _____

   bedroom = _____

9. class = _____

   room = _____

   classroom = _____

10. over = _____

    seas = _____

    overseas = _____

Cockroaches Become Robots

TOKYO, JAPAN—What do you do when you see a cockroach? Do you hit it with a newspaper? Do you say, "Oh, yuck!" and go for the bug spray? Do you step on it?

When researchers at Tokyo University see a cockroach, they take the remote control and make the roach turn around, run left or right, or go forward. These scientists are changing the roaches into robots. Each roach has a tiny backpack that has in it a microprocessor and an electrode set. Then researchers can send signals from the remote control to the backpack. The signals control the movements of the cockroaches.

Why does anyone want to control a cockroach? "Insects can do many things that people can't," says Isao Shimoyama, head of bio-robot research at Tokyo University. In a few years, he says, these robot bugs will carry mini-cameras. They will be able to crawl through earthquake rubble to look for people or slip under doors to spy on someone.

This may seem strange, but the Japanese government thinks the research is very important. The government is giving the scientists $5 million for this research.

First, the researchers breed hundreds of cockroaches. They use only the American cockroach because it is bigger and stronger than other roaches. Then they choose the best roaches and remove their wings and antennae. They put tiny backpacks where the antennae were. The backpacks weigh about three grams, or about two times the weight of the roaches themselves. "Cockroaches are very strong," says Ralph Holzer, who is a researcher at Tokyo University. "They can lift 20 times their own weight."

With a remote control, the scientists send signals to the backpacks. When a roach feels the electricity, it moves. The problem is that the roaches don't always move in the right direction. The researchers are still working on getting the "bugs" out of the electrodes.

▶ **Comprehension questions.**

Discuss the answers to these questions with your classmates.

1. What are scientists changing cockroaches into?

   _____

2. Why do they want to make roaches into robots?

   _____

3. What kinds of things can roaches do to help people?

   _____

4. What do they put on the back of each cockroach?

   _____

5. What is in the tiny backpack?

   _____

6. Why do they use American cockroaches?

   _____

7. What problem do the researchers have?

   _____

8. This reading has another word for *cockroach*. What is it?

   _____

9. There is also another word for *insect*. What is it?

   _____

10. "Get the bugs out" is an idiom that Americans often use. What do you think it means?

    _____

Give your own opinion about these questions.

1. Why do you think cockroaches are better for this kind of work than other insects?

_____

2. Why do you think the scientists are using cockroaches as robots instead of making machine robots?

_____

INSIDE THE NEWSPAPER

▶ Charts and Graphs.

Charts and graphs help newspaper readers to see facts easily and quickly. Look at the graph and answer the questions.

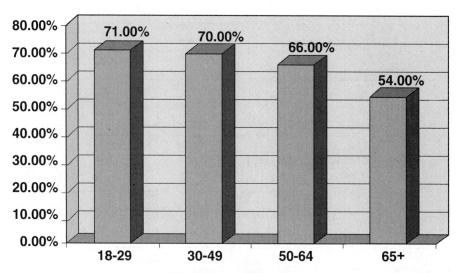

Most people use computers

Percentages of American workers who use a
computer at their jobs, by age groups:

Source: John J. Heldrich Center for Workforce Development

1. What is the title of the graph?
2. What do the numbers at the bottom of the graph show?

3. Which age group uses computers the least?
4. What percentage of workers aged 18-29 use computers at work?
5. Do you think that these percentages will go up or go down in the future? Explain your answer.

Now find a chart or a graph in an actual newspaper. With a partner, discuss the information in the graph. Write four questions about it. Then exchange graphs and questions with another group. Answer the other group's questions.

WRITE ALL ABOUT IT

Make a graph about your class. Show the percentage of students from each country, show how many men and how many women there are in the class, or show the ages of the students.

WRAP UP

Design your own robot. Draw a picture of it and label the parts. Write or tell about it. What is it made of? How big is it? What can it do? How can you control it?

Chapter 6

NEIGHBOR CHILDREN ARE MIGHTY HEROES

BEFORE YOU READ

▶ **Use what you know.**

Think about the following three types of heroes. Who are some more examples of each type?

National Heroes	Popular Heroes	Everyday Heroes
Abraham Lincoln	*Michael Jordan*	*firefighter*
Mahatma Gandhi	*Batman*	*Red Cross volunteer*

Find the definition of *hero* in an English dictionary. How do the people in the list fit the definition? What do they have in common? Why are they heroes?

▶ **Make a guess.** Look at the picture on page 55 and at the headline below. Then answer these questions.

1. How old do you think the children in the picture are?
2. Who is the hero in this story?
3. What is the relationship between the children and the man?
4. What heroic thing do you think the children did?

▶ **Find the answers.** Now read the story. Think about these questions.

1. What happened to Gary Lewis?
2. Who came to help him?
3. Who called 911, and why?
4. How was Gary Lewis able to get out from under the car?
5. How do the children feel about what they did?
6. Write one question that you have about the story.

_____ ?

READING

Neighbor Children Are Mighty Heroes

1   DENVER, COLORADO—What does it take to be a **hero**? Muscles? **Courage**? A Superman suit? In the case of five Denver children, it only takes a cry for help. Here's the story of these five heroes as Gary Lewis, the man they helped, tells it.

2   "I like to work on my old '68 Ford. It's my hobby. I wanted to put a new transmission in the car. I put the car up on blocks because I wanted to get under it. I was trying to get the old transmission out when **suddenly** the car moved forward and fell off the blocks. It came down on my **chest**. I couldn't **breathe**.

3   "I tried to yell for help for about five minutes, but I could hardly breathe. Could anyone hear me? Was I going to die? Then all of a sudden I heard some little kids from the **neighborhood**. They were running to the car and saying, 'What happened, mister?'

4   " 'Get help, please. I can't breathe,' I told them. One of the kids ran to his house and told his mom to call 911. Then, before I knew what was happening, all of the kids were around the car. They used every **muscle** in their bodies to lift the car, and I was able to **slide** out from under it."

5   Lewis got out from under the car with just a few **bruises** and cuts. He didn't even have to go to the hospital. "These kids are my heroes," he says. "I don't know how they did it, but I am lucky to be **alive**."

6   Two of the kids have ideas about why they were able to lift the car. "I drink milk," Shugey 1Shead, eight years old, says. "I drink milk, too, and I eat cheese," says Tamika Brown, nine years old. Raymond Brown, father of two of the children, is very proud of them. "We go to church, and we try to teach them to do the right thing. This shows we're doing it the right way, I guess," he says.

7   What do the kids think?

8   Shugey speaks for all of them when he shows his muscles and says, "I feel like a mighty hero."

AFTER YOU READ

▶ Check your understanding.

Write *true* or *false* for each of these sentences. Write each false sentence correctly.

Example: *false*   Gary Lewis has a new Ford.
                         Gary Lewis has a 1968 Ford.

_____ 1. Gary Lewis put his car up on blocks because he didn't want to drive it again.

_____

_____ 2. Gary Lewis likes to work on his car.

_____

_____ 3. The neighbor children didn't hear Gary when he called for help.

_____

_____   4. All the kids ran to ask someone to call 911.

_____

_____   5. Lewis was not badly injured.

_____

Circle the letter of the best answer.

1. The car fell off the blocks because
   a. the kids pushed it.
   b. it moved forward by itself.
   c. Gary Lewis moved the blocks.

2. Gary Lewis couldn't breathe because
   a. there was a heavy car on top of him.
   b. he was running very fast.
   c. he has a lung disease.

3. Lewis was able get out from under the car when
   a. the children worked together to lift it up a little bit.
   b. the paramedics came and pulled him out.
   c. he pushed the car forward.

4. Raymond Brown is
   a. a doctor from the hospital.
   b. someone from the neighborhood church.
   c. the father of two of the kids.

5. The word *mighty* probably means
   a. afraid.   b. powerful.   c. weak.

Write answers for these questions.

1. How many children does the story talk about?

_____

2. What is Gary's hobby?

   _____

3. How long did Gary try to call for help before the children came?

   _____

4. According to Shugey, why could he help to lift a car?

   _____

5. How old is Tamika Brown?

   _____

Think about the information in the story. Use your own ideas to answer these questions.

1. What makes someone a hero?

   _____

   _____

2. Do you think that the children should receive a reward for what they did? Explain your answer.

   _____

   _____

3. Why was Mr. Brown proud of his children?

   _____

   _____

4. How did Gary Lewis feel about what happened?

   _____

   _____

FIND THE MEANING

▶ **Vocabulary.** Match each of these words from the story with the best definition.

_____ 1. hero (n.)	a. move smoothly
_____ 2. courage (n.)	b. the upper front part of the body
_____ 3. muscle (n.)	c. quickly and unexpectedly
_____ 4. suddenly (adv.)	d. a person who does something brave to help others
_____ 5. chest (n.)	
_____ 6. breathe (v.)	e. the ability to do something dangerous without being afraid
_____ 7. neighborhood (n.)	f. living, not dead
_____ 8. slide (v.)	g. take air into the body
_____ 9. bruise (n.)	h. a black-and-blue mark on the skin
_____ 10. alive (adj.)	i. an area near a particular place
	j. a part of the body that tightens or stretches to make other body parts move

▶ **Cloze.**

Fill in each blank with the correct vocabulary word from the story.

immediately	alive	courage	heroes	lucky
neighbor	kids	thankful	proud	right

Pretend that Gary Lewis is writing to the father of two of the children.

Dear Raymond,

I would like to tell you again how _____ I am to your children

for saving my life. They and their friends are wonderful _____ . They

are still very young, but they have a lot of _____ . They are not afraid

to do the _____ thing. When they heard that I needed help, they

didn't stop to think about themselves. They came _____ to rescue me.

I am a very _____ man. Because of these children, I am

_____ today. You should be very _____ to be their father,

and I am very proud to be your _____ . Your children are truly young

_____ .

Sincerely,

Gary

IMPROVE YOUR READING

▶ **Main ideas.** The main idea of a paragraph tells what the paragraph is about. It talks about the whole paragraph, but it does not include any ideas that are not in the paragraph.

Example:

Which is the best main idea for paragraph 1?
a. There are many heroes in the world.
b. Gary Lewis is a hero because he saved five children.
c. Five children are heroes because they helped Gary Lewis.

Explanation: Sentence a. is not a good main idea because it is too general. The paragraph is about these five heroes, not all the heroes in the world. Sentence b. is not a good main idea because it is not true. Sentence c. is the best main idea because it tells who the heroes are and why they are heroes.

Circle the letter of the best main idea for the other paragraphs in the reading.

1. Paragraph 2
    a. Gary's car fell on him and he couldn't breathe.
    b. Gary is a professional mechanic.
    c. Most people are very careful when they repair a car.

2. Paragraph 3
    a. Gary couldn't talk at all.
    b. Some neighbor children came to help Gary Lewis when they heard him calling for help.
    c. The kids are little.

3. Paragraph 4

   a. The children lifted up the car, and Gary got out from under it.

   b. All the children ran to call 911.

   c. All parents should teach their children to call 911 in emergencies.

4. Paragraph 5

   a. Gary had to stay in the hospital for a long time.

   b. Gary is thankful because the children saved him and he isn't badly hurt.

   c. Gary doesn't know how the kids lifted the car.

5. Paragraph 6

   a. Shugey is eight years old.

   b. Children should drink milk.

   c. The children are proud of themselves, and Raymond Brown is proud of them too.

EXTRA! EXTRA READING!

Falling Boy Bounces Off Woman

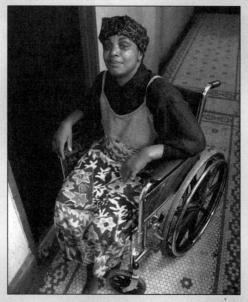

NEW YORK—A woman in a wheelchair became a hero when a two-year-old boy fell from a third-floor window into her lap.

Barbara Jones is the hero. She is a 31-year-old woman who is unable to walk. Ms. Jones was visiting her mother in Harlem, a New York City neighborhood. She was sitting in her wheelchair in a favorite place outside her mother's apartment building. "I was sitting in the sunshine talking to a friend," she said. "When I come to visit my mother, I have a favorite place where I like to sit and talk to the neighbors. It was in the middle of July, and the sun was very hot.

We decided to go to a place on the other side of the building. I don't usually like to sit there because it's so noisy. But there I was! Suddenly something very strange happened."

Above her, on the third floor of the building, Adonis Gomez was playing. He was jumping on a sofa with his cousin. The sofa was near an open window.

"I was cooking in the kitchen," his mother said. "It got too hot, so I opened the window in the living room. It was the only window that did not have a grate on it."

"I can jump higher than you can," Adonis said to his cousin. Adonis took a big jump, but he didn't come back down on the sofa. Instead, he bounced out the open window. He fell three stories. His arms hit Ms. Jones' head. Then he rolled across her lap and fell to the ground next to her wheelchair.

Adonis was hurt, but he was not dead. An ambulance took him to the hospital. Ms. Jones had only a small cut near her left eye. "Now I know God had a reason for me to move to that side of the building," Ms. Jones said.

▶ Comprehension questions.

Work with a partner. Discuss the answers to these questions about the story.

1. Where was Barbara Jones sitting?
2. Why did she go to the other side of the building?
3. Where was Adonis?
4. What was he doing?
5. Where was his mother?
6. Why was the window open?
7. What happened when Adonis jumped from the sofa? Where did he land?
8. Did Adonis die when he fell three stories?
9. Do you think that Barbara Jones is a hero? Explain your answer.
10. How is the story about Adonis similar to the story about Gary Lewis?

INSIDE THE NEWSPAPER

▶ Today's horoscope.

A horoscope gives you a forecast of the future. Your birth date tells you what sign you are. Read these horoscopes and work in pairs on the questions below.

AQUARIUS (Jan. 20-Feb. 19)
Something will happen today that will give you extra money in your pocket.

PISCES (Feb. 20-March 20)
Friends will bring you happiness today.

ARIES (March 21-April 19)
Be careful of something or someone falling from a high building.

TAURUS (April 20-May 20)
You will be lucky today if you will look at everything closely.

GEMINI (May 21-June 20)
Someone who likes you may tell you today. Don't be surprised if love comes to your door.

CANCER (June 21-July 22)
If you work with machines, be very careful. You could be hurt.

LEO (July 23-Aug. 22)
Are you working hard or trying to learn something new? Today may be the day that you have success in your work or your learning.

VIRGO (Aug. 23-Sept.22)
Your happy outlook on life will help one of your friends who is sad.

LIBRA (Sept. 23-Oct. 23)
This is a good day to work with friends or neighbors. You may save a life.

SCORPIO (Oct. 24-Nov. 22)
Someone you have just met will be important in your life later this month.

SAGITTARIUS (Nov. 23-Dec. 21)
Wake up early today. The morning hours will be very important.

CAPRICORN (Dec. 22-Jan. 19)
Love is coming your way, so open your eyes and look for it.

1. Tell your partner when you were born and what your horoscope for today says.

   I was born on _____ . My horoscope says _____

   _____

2. Is your horoscope true for today?

   _____

3. Which horoscope fits the story "Falling Boy Bounces Off Woman"?

   _____

4. Two horoscopes tell about what happened in "Neighbor Children Are Mighty Heroes." Which ones are they?

   _____   _____

Find your horoscope in an actual newspaper. Do you agree with what it says? Why or why not?

WRITE ALL ABOUT IT

What happened to you yesterday? Write a horoscope for yesterday. Start with your sign and the dates.

WRAP UP

Talk with your classmates about these questions.
1. The first story tells about neighbor children who were heroes. Are you a hero?
2. Do you know someone who is a hero? Tell about the person.
3. What makes a person a hero?
4. It is 2 A.M. You are driving home from a party. The car in front of you goes off the road and hits a tree. What do you do?

Chapter 7

GORILLA SAVES LITTLE BOY

BEFORE YOU READ

▶ **Discussion questions.** Talk about these questions with your classmates.

1. Have you been to the zoo in your country or in the city you live in now? What do you like about the zoo? Which animals are your favorites?
2. What is a gorilla? Describe this animal.
3. Are gorillas intelligent? How are gorillas and human beings alike?

▶ **Make a guess.** Look at the picture of the gorillas at the Brookfield Zoo.

1. What do you see in the photo?
2. What are the gorillas doing?

▶ **Find the answers.** Now read the story. Think about these questions.

1. How old is the little boy?
2. How did he get into the gorilla pit?
3. Who is Binti Jua?
4. What did Binti Jua do?
5. Who took Bobby from Binti Jua's arms?

READING

Gorilla Saves Little Boy

1 BROOKFIELD, ILLINOIS—A mother gorilla at the Brookfield Zoo saved the life of a little boy. The three-year-old boy, Bobby, visited the **zoo** with his mother and father. First, they looked at the lions. Bobby's father took a photo of the mother lion and her babies, but Bobby ran to the gorilla pit. He **heard** the gorillas, but he couldn't see them.

2 He climbed over the **fence** and looked down. There were seven gorillas in the pit. Bobby was scared. "Mommy," he cried. Bobby tried to hold on to the top of the fence, but his hand **slipped**. He fell 27 feet onto the **concrete** floor of the gorilla **pit**. He **hit** his head on the hard concrete and did not move. The gorillas came to look at the little boy. Bobby's mother screamed, "Help! My **son** is in the pit. The gorillas will kill him."

3 Two **paramedics** heard Bobby's mother. They ran to see what had happened. They looked down into the pit. They saw Bobby on the floor. They also saw a mother gorilla with a baby on her back. She had her hand on Bobby's head.

4 A zoo worker said, "That's Binti Jua. What will she do to the little boy?" The zoo worker and the paramedics ran down to a door that opened into the pit. Binti Jua carefully picked up Bobby and pushed the other gorillas aside. She carried him to the door and put him down very gently. The zoo worker and the paramedics opened the door. They took Bobby out of the pit and took him to a hospital.

5 Many people heard about Binti Jua and the little boy. One woman sent a gift to Binti Jua. It was a perfect **gift** for a gorilla—25 pounds of bananas.

AFTER YOU READ

▶ Check your understanding.

Write *true* or *false* for each of these sentences. Write each false sentence correctly.

Example: <u>*false*</u>   Bobby went to the zoo with a friend.
<u>*Bobby went to the zoo with his mother and father.*</u>

_____ 1. Bobby climbed over a fence to see the lions.

_____

_____ 2. Bobby fell 27 feet into the gorilla pit.

_____

_____ 3. Two paramedics and a zoo worker went to the door in the gorilla pit.

_____

_____ 4. Binti Jua is a mother gorilla.

_____

_____ 5. Binti Jua hurt Bobby because she was very rough with him.

_____

Circle the letter of the best answer.

1. The zoo in the story is in
   a. Denver, Colorado.
   b. Brookfield, Illinois.
   c. Los Angeles, California.
2. Bobby climbed the fence because
   a. he could hear but not see the gorillas.
   b. he didn't like the lions.
   c. he could see but not hear the gorillas.
3. Binti Jua was
   a. dangerous.
   b. kind.
   c. hungry.

4. Bobby did not move because

    a. he hit his head on the concrete.

    b. he was afraid.

    c. he was sleepy.

5. Binti Jua's present was

    a. peanuts.

    b. toys.

    c. bananas.

Write answers to these questions.

1. Who is Bobby?

_____

2. How old is Bobby?

_____

3. What is Binti Jua?

_____

4. How does Bobby get into the gorilla pit?

_____

5. Where is the zoo?

_____

Now write five more questions of your own.

1. _____

2. _____

3. _____

4. _____

5. _____

FIND THE MEANING

▶ **Vocabulary.** Match each of these words from the story with the best definition.

_____ 1. zoo (n.)   a. a present that you give to someone

_____ 2. hear (v.)   b. a deep hole

_____ 3. fence (n.)   c. strike

_____ 4. slip (v.)   d. a boy child of a mother and father

_____ 5. concrete (n.)   e. a place to keep wild animals

_____ 6. paramedic (n.)   f. listened to

_____ 7. pit (n.)   g. cement mixture used to make buildings

_____ 8. son (n.)   h. slide and fall

_____ 9. gift (n.)   i. a person who helps a doctor or nurse

_____ 10. hit (v.)   j. something we use to keep people or
                                           animals out

▶ **Cloze.** Fill in each blank with the correct vocabulary word from the story.

mother	saved	took	fell	workers	gorilla
baby	zoo	pit			

Binti Jua was born at a large _____ . When the baby gorilla was only three days old, her mother became very sick. She could not feed her baby. The zoo workers were very worried. They were afraid the little gorilla would die, so one of the _____ took the baby gorilla home to his wife.

The wife of the zoo worker fed the baby _____ every two hours with a bottle. She held the baby and kept it clean. She played with the _____ , too. In other words, she became Binti Jua's _____ .

When Binti Jua was older, the zoo worker _____ her back to the zoo. She learned to live with other gorillas, but she always remembered the kind woman who _____ her life by feeding her and caring for her.

Some people think that Binti Jua was kind to the little boy who _____ into the gorilla _____ because she had been fed and loved by a human mother.

IMPROVE YOUR READING

▶ **Scanning.** Scanning is reading very quickly to find specific information. For example, when you want to rent an apartment, you do not read every advertisement in the paper carefully. Instead, you scan to find the apartments in the location where you want to live.

Look at the reading about the gorilla again. Scan it to find the answers to these questions as fast as you can.

1. What is the name of the zoo?
2. How many gorillas were there in the pit?
3. How far did Bobby fall?
4. What was the mother gorilla's name?
5. How many pounds of bananas did the gorilla receive?

EXTRA! EXTRA READING

Man Saves E-Mail Friend

EL PASO, TEXAS — One morning in April, Jim Reed checked his e-mail. He found a strange message on the e-mail. It was from a woman in Pittsburgh, Pennsylvania. He had talked to her on e-mail many times in the last ten days. All the other messages were fun and interesting to read. This message was different.

The message said, "Good-bye loved kowihn yu I amj leavig."

Mr. Reed was frightened by the message. He tried to under-stand the words that were not spelled right. He quickly wrote a message to his new friend.

"What do you mean by the message you just sent me?"

He waited but did not get an answer. He wrote back, "Please talk to me."

Finally, she wrote, "I am falllljg asleep waht ti say gildgye ti ny friends." Mr. Reed thought hard about this message. "Is she going to kill herself?" he thought.

"What is your phone number?" he typed. The woman sent a phone number. Mr. Reed called. At first the phone was busy. Then it just rang and rang. He called directory assistance in Pittsburgh. They connected him with the police. Reed told his story. Then he faxed them what his friend wrote.

The police and paramedics quickly went to thei woman's house. When she didn't answer the doorbell, they broke in. They found her on the floor near the computer. She told them, "I took 60 pills." The paramedics rushed her to the hospital.

"Mr. Reed did a great job of saving this woman," the police captain said. "If he hadn't guessed at the e-message, she would be dead now." The woman is fine now, and she thanks Mr. Reed for saving her life.

▶ Comprehension questions.

1. How did Mr. Reed meet his new friend?
2. Did he ever see her?
3. How long did they write e-mail to each other?
4. What was different about the e-mail message this time?
5. What do you think her e-mail message that begins with Good-bye said?
6. What message was the most important one that Mr. Reed sent?
7. How did this message help him save her life?
8. How did the woman try to kill herself?
9. Was she glad that Mr. Reed saved her?
10. The story about Binti Jua is about a gorilla and a little boy. Mr. Reed's story is different, but it is also like the Binti Jua story. How are the two stories similar?
11. Do you think that some animals have the same feelings as people do?

INSIDE THE NEWSPAPER

▶ Headlines.

A headline is the words in large letters above a newspaper story, such as **Gorilla Saves Little Boy.** A headline gives the main idea of a story. It usually has a subject, a verb, and an object. Read each headline below and tell the class what you think the newspaper story will talk about.

1. **Gunmen Rob Bank**
2. **Russian Skater Wins at Olympics**
3. **Fire Destroys Apartment Building**
4. **President Speaks to Nation**
5. **Gang Leader Is in Jail**

WRITE ALL ABOUT IT

Choose one of the five headlines. Write one or two sentences that tell who did what, when, and where. Also write why it happened. Give details, so your readers will "see" what happened. In a newspaper, the *who, what, when, where,* and sometimes *why* and *how* are called the lead.

WRAP UP

Prepare to talk to your classmates or write about one of these topics.

1. Have you ever saved an animal or a person? Or have you ever helped to save someone? Tell what happened.
2. Do you think that zoos are good places to keep animals? Why or why not?
3. Do you use e-mail? Who are your e-mail friends? Do you like to use e-mail more than you like to use the telephone?

Chapter 8

BASKETBALL STARS BECOME HIP-HOP SINGERS

BEFORE YOU READ

▶ **Use what you know.** In small groups, brainstorm about hip-hop or rap music. Each person tells the group anything that he/she can think of about the topic. One person should write a list of ideas. Then each group shares its ideas with the whole class.

▶ **Make a guess.** Look at the title and the photo. Answer these questions.

1. Which sport does the article talk about?
2. What is hip-hop?
3. What, besides basketball, are these players famous for?
4. Who is Shaquille O'Neal?

◗ **Find the answers.** Think about these questions as you read the story.

1. What is the NBA?
2. What kind of music do many of the players write and perform?
3. What is one reason that hip-hop is popular with NBA players?
4. What do rap singers usually look like?
5. What did Shaquille O'Neal talk about in one of his songs?

READING

Basketball Stars Become Hip-Hop Singers

1   LOS ANGELES, CALIFORNIA—Can a star basketball player also be a star hip-hop singer? If you ask Shaquille O'Neal and some of his National Basketball Association (NBA) buddies, they'll say "Sure!"

2   In the NBA, hip-hop music is as **common** as the jump shot. Hip-hop is similar to rap music and is especially **popular** with young African Americans. This music is played in locker rooms before basketball games and in **arenas** during halftime. Many of the players, like Shaquille O'Neal of the Los Angeles Lakers, write rap **rhymes** when they travel on airplanes from one city to another. Some of the players even have rap radio shows, and others **perform** in music videos.

3   The NBA has a closer **connection** to hip-hop than any other sports league. This is partly because of the large number of African-American players, but also because the basketball league just loves hip-hop. Every February, the NBA invites popular rap singers to perform at its All-Star weekend. Two rap songs, Kurtis Blow's classic of the 1980s "Basketball" and Naughty by Nature's "Hip-Hop Hooray," are on the league's 50th **anniversary** video.

4   When they play basketball, some of the younger **stars** even try to look like hip-hop singers. Like rap stars, they don't smile in photographs and videos. They try to upset the players on the other team by looking tough. They wear **scowls** that show they are rebels. "Hip-hop is just part of a lot of the athletes' culture," says Kerry Kittles, a player on the New Jersey Nets team. "All of us grew up listening to rap and playing basketball, and the rappers grew up doing the same thing. A lot of players want to be rappers, and a lot of rappers would like to be players."

5   Master P. is a famous rap star who wants to be a basketball player. Two NBA teams, the Charlotte Hornets and the Toronto Raptors, have invited him to their training camps. They enjoy listening to his music, but many people think that he is not good enough at basketball to be on an NBA team.

6   Shaquille O'Neal, whose nickname is Shaq, is the greatest example of an NBA player who became a rapper. He has made four successful rap albums. One of his rap songs, "It Was All a Dream," tells how he felt when he became successful.

"... somebody wake me up this can't be real
lookin' in the paper, Shaq's about to make a hundred mil
somebody smack me, it's gotta be fake
20,000-square-foot crib on the back of a lake . . ."

7   Both basketball and rap music have brought Shaq this **success**.

AFTER YOU READ

▶ **Check your understanding.**

Write *true* or *false* for each of these sentences. Rewrite each false sentence correctly.

_____   1. Shaquille O'Neal is a famous football player.

_____   2. Hip-hop is a special kind of basketball game.

_____   3. Kurtis Blow is a rap singer.

_____   4. Shaquille O'Neal's nickname is Rapper.

_____   5. Shaq's song "It Was All a Dream" is about being in love.

Complete the sentences with information from the story.

1. The team that Shaquille O'Neal plays for is the _____ .

2. The NBA invites well-known rap singers to perform at its All-Star weekend every _____ _____ .

3. The rap song "Basketball" was written by _____ .

4. The Charlotte Hornets and the Toronto Raptors have invited _____ to their training camps.

5. One of Shaquille O'Neal's hip-hop songs is called _____ .

Write answers to these questions. Work with a partner. Compare your answers, and discuss any answers that are different.

1. Do the players of the NBA think that they can be excellent basketball players and famous hip-hop singers?

   _____

2. When can you hear rap music at an NBA game?

   _____

3. What do many basketball players do while they are flying on airplanes?

   _____

4. Why is hip-hop especially popular with NBA players?

   _____

5. Who is Kurtis Blow?

   _____

6. Why do some of the younger basketball players not try to smile or look friendly in photographs?

   _____

7. What is the name of a successful rap singer who would like to be a basketball player?

   _____

8. What is the name of a famous basketball player who is also a successful rap star?

   _____

Give your own opinion about these questions.

1. How did Shaquille O'Neal feel when he became a success?

   _____

2. Would Shaquille O'Neal be famous as a hip-hop singer if he were not a famous basketball player?

   _____

FIND THE MEANING

▶ **Vocabulary.** Match each word from the story with the best definition. Be sure to pay attention to the part of speech for each word.

_____ 1. star (n.)

_____ 2. common (adj.)

_____ 3. arena (n.)

_____ 4. rhyme (n.)

_____ 5. perform (v.)

_____ 6. connection (n.)

_____ 7. popular (adj.)

_____ 8. anniversary (n.)

_____ 9. scowl (n.)

_____ 10. success (n.)

a. achievement; things happening in the way that you want them to

b. facial expression of anger

c. entertain people by acting, singing, or dancing

d. found everywhere

e. well-liked by many people

f. a singer, actor, or athlete who is very famous

g. something that is associated with something else

h. open place with seats in it where people can watch sports

i. two lines of a song or poem that end with the same sound

j. celebration of the date when something important happened

▶ **Cloze.**

Fill in each blank with the correct vocabulary word from the story.

basketball (n.)	famous (adj.)	joined (v.)	team (n.)	song (n.)
connection (n.)	nickname (n.)	wanted (v.)	signed (v.)	star (n.)

Shaquille O'Neal is both a big man, more than 7 feet tall and 310 pounds, and a big basketball _____ . Here are some facts about this _____ athlete. He was born March 6, 1972, in Newark, New Jersey. His _____ , Shaq, is taken from his full name, Shaquille Rashaun, which means "little warrior" in Arabic. When he was a child, he did not want to play _____ or be a rap singer. He _____ to be a break dancer, but when he was 13, he started playing basketball for an American _____ in Germany, where he was living with his family. In Germany, he met Dale Brown, the coach of the basketball team of Louisiana State University (LSU). This _____ with Coach Brown led Shaq to choose LSU after he finished high school. Then, at the age of 20, Shaq _____ the Orlando Magic, an NBA team. Shaq is now number 34 with the Los Angeles Lakers and has _____ a 7-year contract for $123 million, or "a hundred mil" as Shaquille calls it in his rap _____ "It Was All a Dream." What an amazing success story he has had!

IMPROVE YOUR READING

▶ **Punctuation.**

Punctuation marks and capital letters can help you to understand what you are reading.

Capital letters are used at the beginning of a sentence and for proper nouns. In paragraph 1, every sentence begins with a capital letter. *Shaquille O'Neal* is capitalized because it is the name of a person, and each word in *National Basketball Association* begins with a capital letter because it is the name of an organization.

A period (.) shows where a statement ends. In paragraph 2, every sentence ends with a period.

A question mark (?) lets us know that a sentence is a question. We can see that the first sentence in paragraph 1 is a question because there is a question mark at the end of it.

A comma (,) can come between the parts of a long (compound or complex) sentence. In paragraph 1, the comma after the word *buddies* separates the two parts of the sentence.

An apostrophe (') shows that some letters are left out of a word, or that a noun is possessive (showing ownership). In paragraph 1, *they'll* is a short way of saying *they will*. In paragraph 3, the apostrophe in Kurtis Blow's tells us that the song is his.

Quotation marks (" ") show that we are reading exactly what someone says. We also use quotation marks for the title of a song or story. In paragraph 1, there are quotation marks around *Sure* to show that this is what the players say. In paragraph 3, the word *Basketball* has quotation marks because it is the name of a song.

Use the punctuation to help you to answer these questions about the story.

1. In paragraph 2, why is there a comma in this sentence? *Some of the players even have rap radio shows, and others perform in music videos.*

   _____

2. In paragraph 3, quotation marks are used for the names of two songs. One of them is "Basketball." What is the other song?

   _____

3. In paragraph 4, why are there quotation marks around the last two sentences?

   _____

4. In paragraph 4, what does the apostrophe tell us in this sentence? *Hip-hop is just a part of a lot of the athletes' culture.*

   _____

5. Where is the comma in the last sentence in paragraph 5?

   _____

6. What is the name of the song in paragraph 6?

   _____

Now look at the lines from Shaquille O'Neal's song. Is it easy for you to read? If it isn't, one reason is that writers of songs or poems do not always follow standard punctuation rules.

1. Where should there be capital letters and periods in line 1? Rewrite it correctly here.

   <u>somebody wake me up this can't be real</u>

   _____

2. In the second line, what is the complete spelling for *lookin'*?

   _____

3. What does *Shaq's* stand for in line 2?

   _____

4. Where should there be capital letters and periods in line 3? Rewrite it correctly here.

   <u>somebody smack me, it's gotta be fake</u>

   _____

EXTRA! EXTRA READING!

Moms Balance World Cup with Motherhood

The U.S. Women's Soccer Team made history in the summer of 1999. More than 40 million TV viewers saw them win the World Cup against China, but the world didn't see that two of the players had another full-time job. These two soccer stars were also moms.

For most women, it is difficult to work eight hours a day in an office when they have small children. Carla Overbeck and Joy Fawcett play in international games and practice with the team in cities far away from home for six months each year.

How can they be World Cup players and also be good mothers? Balancing these two parts of their lives is not easy.

Joy says, "I grew up in a big family. I love kids, and I wanted to have them early. I never thought that I couldn't do that and have a career, too." Joy and her husband, Walter, who is an engineer, live in California. They planned the births of their two daughters around the soccer season, which begins in January. Joy trained into the ninth month of both her pregnancies. Two weeks after each of her babies was born, she was working out again. At soccer games, her mother, sisters, or a nanny watched the kids. If the baby got hungry, Joy fed her when she wasn't on the field playing.

The captain of the team, Carla, and her husband, Greg, who owns a restaurant in North Carolina, have a son. Joy was an inspiration to Carla. "It really helped me to know that Joy was a mother and still played soccer," she says.

What do their husbands think about their soccer-playing wives? Their husbands are proud of them and help them. "Greg kept our son at home when I was out of the state, but he traveled with him to every game during the World Cup," Carla says. "He's basically Mr. Mom." As for Joy, when she and her kids travel without him, they call their dad every night. She says that they go to sleep more easily after they have talked to him.

The U.S. Women's Soccer Team has become like a large family to Carla's and Joy's children. The other players enjoy watching the kids grow up. The children also keep the team feeling positive when they have hard times. In 1995, when they lost the World Cup in Sweden, one of the kids was just learning to walk. She toddled out onto the field to meet her mom, and everyone in the stadium stood up and clapped. "These kids never let you forget what is really important," Joy says.

▶ Comprehension questions.

1. Which team won the World Cup in women's soccer in 1999?
2. What is unusual about two of the players?
3. How long did Joy wait after she had her babies to begin practicing and training again?
4. Who watched the babies when Joy was playing in a game?
5. Why was Joy Fawcett an inspiration to Carla Overbeck?
6. How do the women's husbands feel about their wives playing soccer?
7. What does Carla mean when she calls her husband "Mr. Mom"?

8. Why did the people in the stadium clap after the U.S. lost its game in 1995?
9. What does Joy mean when she says that the kids never let you forget what is really important?
10. How do you think that the children feel about their moms being soccer stars?

INSIDE THE NEWSPAPER

▶ The Sports Section.

The Sports Section of a newspaper tells readers about many kinds of sports. A sports calendar is usually part of this section of the newspaper. Use the calendar that follows to answer the questions.

SPORTS CALENDAR							
Event	**Today**	**Sun.**	**Mon.**	**Tues.**	**Wed.**	**Thurs.**	**Fri.**
Super Bowl Football		Atlanta 2 p.m.					
Nuggets Basketball	@ Dallas 8 p.m.						
CU Men's Basketball			Kansas 7 p.m.				Okla. U 7 p.m.
CU Women's Basketball	Ark. 3 p.m.			Okla. State 7:30 p.m.			
Avalanche Hockey	@ St. Louis 7:30 p.m.				@ Vancouver 6 p.m.		
Boxing Jeffers/Kahn	New York 2 p.m.						
Mile High	12:30 and 7 p.m.		12:30 p.m.	12:30 p.m.	12:30 p.m.	12:30 p.m.	7 p.m.

1. How many different sports are listed on the calendar?
2. What is the name of the hockey team?
3. When do the Nuggets play?
4. What are the names of the boxers?

5. On what days of the week do the Mile High Dogs race?
6. What team is playing at Oklahoma State University on Tuesday?
7. Why is *Super Bowl Football* in larger letters?

Now look at a sports calendar in an actual newspaper. Answer these questions.

1. Which sports are listed?
2. How many days are shown on the calendar?
3. What is the name of your favorite team?
4. When will your favorite team play its next game?
5. Where will the next game be?

WRITE ALL ABOUT IT

Write a paragraph about your favorite sport. Is there a team that you like best? Tell why you like the sport and the team.

WRAP UP

Prepare to discuss or write about one of these questions.

1. In Shaquille O'Neal's song, he talks about making $100,000,000. Do you think that professional athletes make too much money? Explain your answer.
2. The second story is about athletes who are mothers of small children. Do you think that it is a good idea for women with young families to have careers? What are the problems for the women? for the children? for their husbands?

 Inside the NEWS

Chapter 9

TITANIC POSTCARD HELPS SAVE A LIFE

BEFORE YOU READ

▶ **Use what you know.** Talk about these questions with your classmates.

1. What do you know about the Titanic? What happened to it?
2. Do you know anyone who likes to collect things such as stamps, coins, or postcards? What kinds of things do people in your country collect? Do they pay a lot of money for these things?
3. Why are people interested in old things? What can they learn from looking at old things?

▶ **Make a guess.** Look at the pictures on page 89 and read the title. Answer these questions.

1. What is there a picture of on the front of the postcard?
2. When did people travel on ships like the Titanic?
3. How old do you think the postcard is?
4. Why is this postcard valuable?
5. How do you think a postcard can help to save someone's life?

▶ **Find the answers.** As you read the story, think about these questions.

1. Who had the postcard?
2. Who signed the postcard?
3. What was the matter with Mary Shelley?
4. Why did Joey decide to sell the postcard?
5. How much money did he get for it?
6. What did he do with the money?

READING

Titanic Postcard Helps Save a Life

1   BALTIMORE, MARYLAND—An old postcard changed the lives of an eleven-year-old boy and a very sick woman. The postcard had a picture of the steamship Titanic. The Titanic was the biggest ocean liner in the world. It hit an **iceberg** and **sank** on April 14, 1912. More than 1500 of the 2200 people on the ship were **killed**.

2   The postcard was passed from one person to another for more than 80 years. Then it **showed up** at a card show for people who like to **collect** postcards. An eleven-year-old boy, Joey Russell, came to the show with his grandfather. His grandfather knew everything about the Titanic and its trip from England to New York. "Let's buy that postcard," he told Joey. "It will be important someday."

3   Two years later, Joey's grandfather took him on a special trip. They went on a cruise ship to the North Atlantic Ocean to watch as workers raised the Titanic up from the bottom of the ocean. Joey put his special postcard in his bag for the trip. On the ship, Joey met Edith Haisman. This woman was on the Titanic when it sank. She was one of the people who were rescued. Joey pulled the postcard out of his pocket. "Please sign this, Mrs. Haisman," he said. She was happy to write her name on the back of the postcard.

4   When Joey got home, he put the postcard away and forgot about it. Then Kate Shelley, one of Joey's friends, told him that her mother, Mary, was very sick. She had <u>leukemia</u>, which is a very serious blood **disease**. She needed an **operation**, but there was a problem. The operation was very <u>expensive</u>, and the family needed $80,000 to pay for it. Friends and <u>relatives</u> tried to help. But where could they get so much money?

5   Then when Joey went to see the new movie "Titanic," he had an idea. "Millions of people are seeing this movie and reading about the Titanic," Joey thought. He remembered the old postcard with Edith Haisman's **signature** on it. "Maybe I can sell it for some money. Then I can help Kate's <u>mom</u>."

6   Joey told his mother and father about his idea to help Mrs. Shelley. His <u>parents</u> helped him try to sell the postcard to the person who would pay the
most money for it. Joey's story was on television and in newspapers. Joey and Kate even went to New York to be on a **national** TV show. After the show, many people **called in** to <u>offer</u> money for the Titanic card. Someone bought it for $60,000.

7   Joey's big heart and the old Titanic postcard worked together to save a woman's life.

AFTER YOU READ

▶ Check your understanding.

Write *true* or *false* for each of these sentences. If you think that the statement is false, explain why you think so.

Example: <u>*false*</u>   The Titanic was a famous airplane.
                          The Titanic was a famous ship.

_____   1. There were about 700 people on the Titanic who did not die when it sank.

_____

_____   2. The Titanic arrived in New York on April 14, 1912.

_____

_____   3. Edith Haisman was Joey's grandmother.

_____

_____   4. Kate's mother needed a lot of money to pay for her medical expenses.

_____

_____   5. The popularity of the movie "Titanic" helped to make Joey's postcard worth
              a lot of money.

_____

Scan the reading passage to find the information to complete these statements.

1. The Titanic sank in April _____ .

2. Joey was _____ years old when he went to a card show with his
   grandfather.

3. They raised the Titanic from the _____ Ocean.

4. Mary needed _____ dollars for the operation.

5. Joey and Kate went to _____ to be on a TV show.

**Write answers to these questions. Compare and discuss your answers with your
classmates.**

1. What was the Titanic?

_____

2. Where did it sink?

_____

3. Why did Joey Russell buy a postcard with a picture of the Titanic?

_____

4. Where did Joey go with his grandfather when he was thirteen years old?

_____

5. Who did Joey meet on the cruise ship?

_____

6. What illness did Kate's mother have?

_____

7. How could Joey's postcard help Kate's mother?

_____

Give your opinion about these questions.

1. Why was the postcard worth more money two years after Joey bought it?

_____

2. What did Joey do with the money he got for the postcard? Did he do the right thing?

_____

3. How did Mary Shelley feel about what Joey did for her?

_____

FIND THE MEANING

▶ **Vocabulary.** Match each word from the story with the best definition.

_____	1. iceberg (n.)	a. go to the bottom
_____	2. sink (v.)	b. sickness
_____	3. kill (v.)	c. for the whole nation
_____	4. show up (v.)	d. a person's name written in his/her handwriting
_____	5. collect (v.)	e. communicate by telephone
_____	6. disease (n.)	f. a large, floating piece of ice
_____	7. operation (n.)	g. appear
_____	8. signature (n.)	h. gather from many places
_____	9. national (adj.)	i. end the life of
_____	10. call in (v.)	j. surgery that doctors do to your body to make it healthy

▶ **Cloze.** Fill in each blank with one of the following words.

sign (v.)	again (adv.)	signature (n.)	beautifully (adv.)	television (n.)
wish (v.)	proud (adj.)	postcard (n.)	amazing (adj.)	operation (n.)

This is a letter that Mrs. Haisman might have written to Joey.

Dear Joey,

I was so happy to receive your letter! When we met, I knew that you were a real gentleman. You were so polite when you came up to me and asked me to _____ your postcard. Now I know that you are kind-hearted, too. I'm very _____ of you for selling your Titanic _____ to help your friend's mother. I saw you on _____ when you and Kate went to New York to tell people about the postcard. You spoke _____ when the reporter asked you all those questions.

I'm very glad that my _____ made the postcard more valuable. It's _____ that someone actually paid $60,000 for it, and it is wonderful to know that the money will be used for a good cause.

It is sad that Kate's mother has leukemia. I hope that the _____ will be a success. Please tell Mrs. Shelley that I _____ her a speedy recovery, and please write _____ soon to let me know how things are going.

Sincerely,

Edith Haisman

IMPROVE YOUR READING

▶ Context clues.

Context clues can help you to understand the meaning of a new word. The other words in the sentence and the other sentences in the paragraph are the context. For example, in paragraph 1, you know that an <u>ocean liner</u> is a kind of ship because the sentence before it says that the Titanic was a steamship.

Use the context clues in the reading to help you choose the best meaning for each of these words.

1. Paragraph 2: <u>show</u>
   a. a television program
   b. a place where people can look at and buy things that they like to collect
   c. a place where boats and ships are kept

2. Paragraph 3: <u>raised</u>
   a. tore down
   b. brought up
   c. looked for

3. Paragraph 3: <u>rescued</u>
   a. saved
   b. killed
   c. drowned

4. Paragraph 3: <u>sign</u>
   a. throw away
   b. take
   c. write your name

5. Paragraph 4: <u>leukemia</u>
   a. a lot of money
   b. a blood disease
   c. a problem

6. Paragraph 4: <u>expensive</u>
   a. cheap
   b. easy
   c. costing a lot of money

7. Paragraph 4: <u>relatives</u>
   a. doctors
   b. strangers
   c. people in your family

8. Paragraph 5: <u>mom</u>
   a. mother
   b. friend
   c. family

9. Paragraph 6: <u>parents</u>
   a. mother and father
   b. teachers
   c. friends

10. Paragraph 6: <u>offer</u>
    a. say that you will give
    b. steal
    b. ask for

Canadian Company Wants Icebergs

IQALUIT, CANADA—Many people think that icebergs are big and frightening. They can sink ships and kill people. We don't usually think that they can be useful. However, a company in Newfoundland, Canada, decided that they could make money by using icebergs.

Iceberg Industries is a company in St. John's, Newfoundland. The company makes beer and vodka from the water of icebergs. They even advertise their products with the words: "Made from the water of northern icebergs." Because the weather is very cold in Newfoundland, the company can usually find as much ice as they need near the coast. But for the last few years, the weather has been warmer than usual, and there hasn't been enough ice.

Morris Murphy, a vice-president of Iceberg Industries, had a good idea. He decided to go to Iqaluit, a village in northern Canada, to make a deal with a company there. The name of the company is QC Corporation, and it is owned by Inuit Indians. "We want them to supply icebergs for our beer and vodka," Murphy says. "Iqaluit is a good place to do business. You can be sure there will be a good supply of ice near this town every year." The owners of QC Corporation said "yes" to Iceberg Industries.

But how do you get an iceberg from Iqaluit to Newfoundland? You can't put a rope around an iceberg and pull it thousands of miles. So what can you do?

Michael Brown of the QC Corporation says that sending the ice to Newfoundland won't be a problem. Ships come north every summer, bringing supplies for the people who live in Iqaluit and the area around it. Usually the ships are empty when they go back south. Brown says that they can cut up the icebergs and put the pieces in the empty ships. "We could fill a whole ship with ice from the icebergs," he explains.

This whole business may sound a little strange, but the companies say the first shipments of icebergs to Newfoundland have already begun.

▶ **Comprehension questions.**

1. Why are some people afraid of icebergs?
2. How does Iceberg Industries use icebergs?
3. Why haven't they had enough ice in the last few years?
4. Who is Morris Murphy?
5. Why did he go to Iqaluit?
6. What does he want to buy from the QC Corporation?
7. Why does he think that Iqaluit is a good place for him to do business?
8. How are they going to move the icebergs from Iqaluit to Newfoundland?
9. Do you think that this is a good business idea? Explain.
10. What are some other ways that people can use icebergs?

INSIDE THE NEWSPAPER

▶ **Movie ads.**

Movie ads and listings are part of the Entertainment Section of a newspaper. Read these ads and answer the questions.

★NOW PLAYING

TITANIC

with Leonardo DiCaprio
at the

CLASSIC THEATER

22235 S. College Ave.

"The best movies of all times are at the CLASSIC"

Only $4.00 admission

● ● MOVIE LISTINGS ● ●

Center Mall 12
Dinosaur (PG)
12:00, 2:00, 4:00, 6:00, 8:00

The Plaza 12
The Patriot (R)
1:00, 4:00, 8:00, 10:00

University Hills Theaters 8
The Kid (PG)
1:00, 3:45,
5:30, 8:30

1. What is the name of the theater where "Titanic" is playing?

   _____

2. How much does it cost to see "Titanic"?

   _____

3. I want to see a movie after a late dinner at 8 P.M. Which movie is late in the evening?

   _____

4. What is the name of the movie at the Center Mall?

   _____

5. What do you think the letters *PG* mean after "Dinosaur" and "The Kid"?

   _____

Now find the movie listings in the Entertainment Section of an actual newspaper.

Choose an ad for a movie that looks interesting. Answer these questions.

   1. What is the title of the movie?
   2. What kind of movie is it: action adventure, love story, comedy, thriller?
   3. Who are the main actors?

Look at the movie listings. Answer these questions.

   1. What is the name of the movie theater where you can see the movie that you chose?
   2. What are the times when you can see the movie?

WRITE ALL ABOUT IT

Write about your favorite movie or TV show. Who are the characters? What happens in the movie? Why do you like it?

WRAP UP

Think about the stories in this chapter and prepare to talk with your classmates about one of these topics.

1. Can you think of another well-known disaster in which a lot of people were killed? When and where did it happen? What caused the disaster? Were there any survivors?
2. In the story, Joey helped his friend and her mother by giving them a lot of money to pay their bills. What are other things that family and friends can do to help when someone is seriously ill?
3. If you could meet anyone in the world and ask for his/her signature, who would you most like to meet? Why? What would you say?

Chapter 10

100-Year-Old Woman Becomes U.S. Citizen

BEFORE YOU READ

▶ **Use what you know**. Talk about these questions with your classmates.

1. What is a citizen?
2. Which country are you a citizen of?
3. What is good about being a citizen? What do citizens of a country get that other people in the country do not get?

▶ **Make a guess.** Look at the picture and the title and answer these questions.

1. What country did the woman in the picture come from?
2. How old is she?
3. People from many different countries become citizens of the United States. Why is there a newspaper story about this woman?

▶ **Find the answers.** Now read the story. Think about these questions.

1. How many years did Asano Kanzaki live in the United States before she became a citizen?
2. Why didn't she become a citizen when she first came to the United States?
3. What kind of work did Asano's husband do? What did Asano do?
4. How many children did Asano and Kenichiro have?
5. Why was it easy for the children to become citizens?
6. What happened to the family during World War II?
7. What happened to Akira, the oldest son, during World War II?
8. Why did Asano decide to become a citizen so late in life?

READING

100-Year-Old Woman Becomes U.S. Citizen

1   SEATTLE, WASHINGTON—More than 100 people—young and old—stand up and clap their hands for "a great lady who has always loved America." A **senator** shakes her hand and tells her she is a very important American **citizen**. But the tiny old woman sits quietly at a table, unable to hear many of the nice things everyone is saying about her.

2   Asano Kanzaki is the woman's name. This evening she has become a citizen, 81 years after coming to the United States. Those 81 years have been filled with hard work and life in a **prison camp** during World War II. Those years have also been filled with **raising** a family with **honor** in a new country.

3   Mrs. Kanzaki came to Seattle in September 1917. She married Kenichiro Kanzaki just a few months before she left Japan. At that time, Japanese could not become citizens. They could not own houses. They could not even live in some neighborhoods.

4   Kenichiro worked in a **laundry**. Asano worked raising a family. Their first child, a girl, died when she was just two weeks old. But soon there were other children: five in five years. The children became citizens because they were born in the United States. To them, Japan was a country across the ocean. Japanese was a language they spoke with their parents, not with friends.

5   By 1941, after 24 years in America, the family was doing well in their new country. Then on December 7, 1941, Japan **bombed** Pearl Harbor. The next day Kenichiro was taken to **jail**. Because he was in the Japanese army when he was younger, the U.S. government was afraid he would become a **spy**.

6   A few months later, Asano and her five children joined Kenichiro in a prison camp in Idaho. The whole family lived in a 16 x 20-foot room. By then, the Kanzaki boys were young men. "America is your country, and you must fight for it," their father told them.

7   Akira, the oldest, volunteered for the U.S. Army because of the honor he felt for his family and his country. He was killed in Italy in November 1944. After the war, Asano and her family went back to Seattle. For the first time, Japanese who had come to the U.S. could become citizens if they took classes. She and her husband were working so hard that they did not have time for the classes. As time passed, the children married husbands and wives from different cultures. They were an all-American family.

8   Kenichiro died in 1968, and Asano moved to a small apartment. After her one hundredth birthday, she made a big **decision**. "There's not much time left. I need to become an American citizen." Why now, after so many years? Her youngest son, Hitoshi, says, "Family has always been important to my mother. She comes from a culture that tells you that you must bring honor to your family. Her citizenship brings great honor to her and her family name."

AFTER YOU READ

▶ **Check your understanding.**

Write *true* or *false* for each of these sentences. Rewrite each false sentence correctly.

_____   1. Mrs. Kanzaki understood what people said about her when she became a citizen.

_____

_____   2. Mrs. Kanzaki has lived in the U.S. for 81 years.

_____

_____ 3. She married her husband after she came to the U.S.

_____

_____ 4. She and her husband lived in Honolulu in 1917.

_____

_____ 5. Akira fought in the Japanese army.

_____

Circle the letter of the best answer.

1. Kenichiro died in

   a. 1941.   b. 1944   c. 1968

2. A hundred people clapped their hands when

   a. Asano Kanzaki became a United States citizen.

   b. Asano married Kenichiro.

   c. Asano arrived in Seattle.

3. Her children became United States citizens because

   a. they studied and passed a test.

   b. they married Americans.

   c. they were born in America.

4. When the U.S. and Japan were fighting World War II,

   a. the Kanzaki family went back to Japan.

   b. many Japanese people were sent to prison camps.

   c. Mrs. Kanzaki killed herself.

5. Mrs. Kanzaki wanted to become a citizen because

   a. her husband told her to.

   b. the U.S. government said that she had to.

   c. she wanted to honor her family.

Write the answers to these questions.

1. When did Asano come to the U.S.?

   _____

2. What did Kenichiro do for a living?

   _____

3. What happened on December 7, 1941?

   _____

4. Why did Kenichiro have to go to jail?

   _____

5. Where did the family live during the war?

   _____

6. How did Akira die?

   _____

7. What do you think the expression "an all-American family" in paragraph 7 means?

   _____

8. How old was Asano when she became a citizen of the United States?

   _____

9. Why didn't Mrs. Kanzaki become a citizen when she was younger?

   _____

10. How do you think that her children felt when Mrs. Kanzaki became a citizen?

    _____

FIND THE MEANING

▶ **Vocabulary.** Match each word from the story with the best definition.

_____ 1. senator (n.)   a. a place where clothes are washed

_____ 2. citizen (n.)   b. bring up; help to grow

_____ 3. prison camp (n.)   c. respect

_____ 4. raise (v.)   d. conclusion; result of thinking about a problem

_____ 5. honor (n.)   e. a member of a country by birth or by law

_____ 6. laundry (n.)   f. a place where they keep people from the
                                                           enemy country in a war
_____ 7. bomb (v.)
                                                      g. someone who works in the government to
_____ 8. jail (n.)   make laws

_____ 9. spy (n.)   h. someone who gives secret information to
                                                           another country
_____ 10. decision (n.)
                                                      i. a prison; a place where someone who has
                                                          done something wrong has to stay

                                                      j. attack and destroy a place with explosives

▶ **Cloze.** Fill in each blank with the correct vocabulary word from the story.

grandchildren (n.)   because (conj.)   husbands (n.)   country (n.)   citizen (n.)
government (n.)   Americans (n.)   difficult (adj.)   culture (n.)   died (v.)

This is a letter that Asano Kanzaki might have written to her family.

  "I am very proud to be a _____ of the United States now

_____ I am proud of you, my children and my

_____ . I was very young when I met my husband and came

to this _____ in 1917. Life was very hard at times. We had to

work a lot, and it was _____ to understand the language and

_____ of America. The time during the war was terrible.

People didn't understand that we were not helping the Japanese _____ .

I really hated that camp in Idaho, and I was very sad when Akira _____ .

Later, when my children grew up, got good jobs, and found nice _____

and wives, I was happy for them. Now I see that they are really _____ ,

and I would like to be an American, too.

IMPROVE YOUR READING

▶ Sequencing.

Writers do not always tell the events in a story in the order that they really happened. Putting these events in order can help you understand the story. Number these sentences in the order that they happened in Mrs. Kanzaki's life.

_____ a. Akira, her son, was killed in World War II.

_____ b. The family had to stay in a prison camp.

_____ c. Kenichiro went to jail.

_____ d. Asano Kanzaki became a citizen at the age of 100.

_____ e. Mrs. Kanzaki's children grew up and got married to people who were not Japanese.

_____ f. Mrs. Kanzaki's husband died, and she moved to an apartment.

_____ g. Asano married Kenichiro and came to Seattle.

_____ h. Kenichiro and Asano worked hard and raised a family.

_____ i. The Japanese bombed Pearl Harbor.

EXTRA! EXTRA READING!

Deaf Man Discovers He Can Communicate

MONTE VISTA, COLORADO— Wayne Mix has lived in silence all 81 years of his life. Mr. Mix has never spoken a word. He has never heard a sound.

When he was a child in the 1930s, his family sent him to a school for the deaf and blind. He learned American Sign Language. With American Sign Language, deaf people use their hands to communicate. They can spell words with their fingers, or they can use signs for whole words. Waync communicated with teachers and friends in sign language. He graduated at the age of 20. In those days, people who were deaf did not get jobs and were not part of the community, so Wayne went back to the family farm. His family did not know sign language, so Wayne communicated a little by making simple motions with his hands. He was never able to tell them his thoughts and feelings.

Wayne's father died in 1971. There was no place for Wayne to live, so they sent him to Mountain Meadows nursing home. He was only 51 and much younger and healthier than the other people in the nursing home, but he was treated like the 80- and 90-year-old people because he did not hear or speak. No one knew that Wayne was able to use sign language.

Twenty-nine years passed slowly and silently for Wayne. Then one day he saw a visitor using sign language with her deaf mother during a visit to the nursing home. He walked up to them and signed, "I'm Wayne Mix."

Suddenly everything changed for Wayne. He found many people who knew sign language. He met many of the deaf adults who lived in the little town. These people communicated through sign language, e-mail, television with subtitles and a special telephone that prints the words that are spoken. It was a whole new world for Wayne. Now he could tell people his feelings, his needs, and his thoughts.

The people in Wayne's town were sad about the thousands of days in Wayne's life when no one knew that he could communicate. They wanted to help Wayne to do some of the things he always wanted to do. The workers at the nursing home found out that as a young man he loved to swim, and he loved to see pictures of dolphins swimming. When he started signing again, they asked him where he wanted to go. "Water," Wayne signed.

Mountain Meadows workers had an idea. "Let's send Wayne to Sea World in San Diego." They told other people in town about their idea. Many people in Wayne's town and in other states gave money to help Wayne make the trip. The people at Sea World were very kind to Wayne. They let him swim with the dolphins and help them feed all the sea animals. Newspapers wrote about Wayne, so many people gave money to buy him a special TV and a teletype phone set. These were things Wayne never knew about before.

A whole new world has opened to this man who cannot hear or speak. "We can't change what happened to him for all of those years, but we are trying to make his dreams come true," said one of his new friends.

▶ Comprehension questions.

1. How old is Wayne Mix?
2. Where did he learn American Sign Language?
3. How did he communicate with his family?
4. How old was he when he went to the nursing home?
5. Why did he go to live in the nursing home?
6. How did the workers at the nursing home learn that Wayne could use American Sign Language?
7. How did his life change after he met other deaf people?
8. Why were people sad after Wayne began to communicate?
9. What special thing did Wayne get to do after he began to communicate?
10. In what ways has "a whole new world" opened to Wayne?

INSIDE THE NEWSPAPER

▶ **Sections.**

U.S. newspapers are divided into many sections. Here are the names of some of the sections:

    A. World News
    B. National News
    C. Local News
    D. Editorials
    E. Entertainment
    F. Weather
    G. Obituaries

Discuss the meaning of these words with your classmates. Then match the headlines with the sections where you would find the stories.

_____ 1. **Local Man Wins 1 Million Dollars**

_____ 2. **Academy Awards Tonight on Channel 7**

_____ 3. **Earthquake Hits Village in Turkey**

_____ 4. **U.S. President Says He Will Run Again**

_____ 5. **Warm and sunny today with a high of 75 degrees.**

_____ 6. **Bank President Dies at 96**

_____ 7. **Readers Write Their Opinions on City Traffic**

Look through an actual newspaper. What sections do you find? Is there information about all the sections on the front page or inside the front page?

WRITE ALL ABOUT IT

Write a paragraph about senior citizens, people 60 and older, in your culture. Do they live by themselves or with their families? Do they work? How do they spend their time?

WRAP UP

Prepare to discuss or write about one of these questions.

1. The stories in this chapter are about older people, one who is 81 and another who is 100. Discuss this question with your classmates: Would you like to live to be 100 years old? Why or why not?

2. The second story tells about the life of a man who cannot hear. What are the problems that he has had in his life? If you had to give up seeing or hearing, which would you choose? Why?